My Father's Journey

A Memoir of Lost Worlds
of Jewish Lithuania

My Father's Journey

A Memoir of Lost Worlds of Jewish Lithuania

SARA REGUER

Boston
2015

Library of Congress Cataloging-in-Publication Data:

A catalog record for this book as available from the Library of Congress.

ISBN 978-1-61811-414-3 (hardback)
ISBN 978-1-61811-4150 (electronic)

Cover design by Ivan Grave.

On the cover: Watercolor portrait of Moshe Aron Reguer, entitled "He-Chalutz",
by Thaddeus Rychter, Jerusalem, 1927; Photograph of Simcha Zelig Reguer and
Moshe Aron Reguer, Brest-Litovsk, 1937. Courtesy of Sara Reguer.

Published by Academic Studies Press in 2015

28 Montfern Avenue
Brighton, MA 02135, USA
press@academicstudiespress.com
www.academicstudiespress.com

In Memory of

My parents
Moshe Aron Reguer
Anne Shabasson Reguer

My paternal grandparents
Simcha Zelig Reguer
ראב"ד בריסק דליטא
Sorke Rudensky Reguer

And my aunts and cousins
murdered by the Nazis in
Brest-Litovsk in 1942.

CONTENTS

ACKNOWLEDGEMENTS

This book took years to write in part because of the personal
nature of the material. There are some people who warned me
not to publish it; others urged me to go right ahead. Some people
offered to "do me the favor" of publishing my grandfather's letters
and all of my photographs. The right time has finally arrived
to put it into print.

I owe a debt of gratitude to Rabbi Ezra Y. Schwartz
for helping me understand some of the halakhic issues discussed
in the primary sources. I also want to acknowledge the help
of my copyeditor, Sharona Vedol.

Finally, I want to acknowledge the unfailing support and
encouragement of my family: my husband Raffaele Gershom
Fodde, whose artistic talents are in play in the layout of the
book, and my daughters Dr. Anna-Alexandra Fodde-Reguer and
Elizabeth Ruth Fodde-Reguer, who are the heirs of the burden
of "yichus."

FOREWORD

After my father died, I packed away his letters and documents, figuring that some day, when I had time—well, nearly anyone can finish that sentence, and know what happened next. The time finally arrived two decades later, when my own family was downsizing and I had to go through everything, once and for all. So I found his diplomas, his photographs, his passports, and then a small treasure trove of letters from his family in Brest-Litovsk, written between 1936 and 1941. The most precious to me were those from my grandfather, but the most newsy were from my Aunt Esther. They are written, with one exception, in Yiddish.

At the bottom of one carton were some black, soft-covered notebooks, which seemed to contain a number of Hebrew essays which had been corrected and graded by his professors. I flipped through the first, wondering why my father had kept it, and then found out why: I turned past the last essay, and my heart stopped. On top of the next page was written—in his beautiful Hebrew script—"Hakdama Le-Zikhronotai," "Introduction to My Memoirs." In the spring of 1926, on the eve of his departure for Eretz Yisrael, my father had recorded his experiences until the age of twenty-three.

The memoirs follow the path of a young Lithuanian yeshiva student, immersed in the world of Torah, Talmud, and *musar*—that is, the systematic study of ethics. In describing his experiences, he was a witness to the the yeshiva system during World War I and its aftermath. At first he studied informally in Volozhin, then more formally in a yeshiva run by Rav Isser Zalman Meltzer in Slutzk, and then he traveled to Kremenchug in Ukraine to study in Rav Finkel's—known as the "Alter"—branch of Slobodka Yeshiva, Knesset Israel. In Kremenchug, and in nearby Karilov, he survived three major pogroms and various life-threatening illnesses. There are few surviving first-hand accounts of pogroms and pandemics.

The memoirs describe my father's exposure to the politics of the time, the lure of *Haskala*, or Enlightenment, the rigidity of the yeshiva system, and the final confrontation between yeshiva administrators and a young man who wanted more than just a Torah education.

Memoirs are selective in that the author chooses what to write about, but these choices also reflect what is important to the writer. Thus, what is left out is almost as important as what is included. In the case of my father's story, these omissions are supplemented by the interviews he gave much later in life and stories that have been related to me over the years. I was always interested in the missing people of his past, namely the women in the family, the social structure of Lithuanian Jewry, and family life in "the old country."

So there are letters, memoirs, stories, interviews, and photographs. How to organize this book was a major problem—should it be arranged chronologicially? Or ought each primary source to be placed separately? Should there be historical analysis of each item? In the end, I decided to let the material speak for itself as much as possible, with my comments and explanations—in a different type-face—run in with the text, which I arranged, for the most part, chronologically. I know that I like a straightforward story with as few digressions as possible, and have attempted to provide the same for the reader.

Why did a twenty-three-year-old write his memoirs?

It turns out that what my father wrote is not strictly a memoir, but a kind of autobiography that bridged into a memoir. According to scholars, the critical issues in an autobiography include a description of one's inner life; a confession-like tone; and a realization that the narrator is both the teller and the subject. The autobiographies written by Eastern European Jews in the late nineteenth century typically described a loss of faith and were written by brilliant adolescent males, who needed to tell their story. Earlier in the century, young men like them had turned to the Haskalah, calling for cultural and social reform. By the end of the century, they were turning to socialism or to a new means of Jewish revival, namely political Zionism.

My father's choice to write in Hebrew was an act of identification with both the Haskalah and those who believed there was a need for educational reform, as well as a nod toward Zionism, which reflected his faith in the future. Again, he was not alone in writing his story: there was even a call via Yiddish newspapers by people like Y. L. Peretz, Yankev Dinezon, S. An-sky, and Simon Dubnov to other Jews, requesting that they record and catalogue their experiences during the First World War, which was seen as a watershed, and to send historical documents to them or to educational and historical institutions for preservation and use by scholars. My father was probably aware of these requests.

While the reflections began as autobiographical, their focus shifts from the writer to the events witnessed as the First World War breaks out, followed by the Russian Revolution and the Russian Civil War. "Zikhronotai" becomes a historical narrative. It develops into one of the windows through which a reader can view Jewish life as it transformed at this crucial juncture of time.

Simcha Zelig Reguer, 1900

Sorke Reguer, 1930

Moshe Aron Reguer
Bar Mitzvah, 1916

Moshe Aron Reguer & sisters,
niece, nephew, 1926

מדרש גבֹה „תחכמני" ביאליסטוק

לזכרון נסיעתו של הרבֹ הראש הגאון מרן ר' שרטה פוליאציק שליט"א לאמריקה
ביאליסטוק, ר"ח חֹב תרפֹ"ב

Takhkemoni, Bialystok, 1922;
Rabbi Polachek (fourth from left),
Moshe Aron Reguer (second row, fourth from left)

Takhkemoni, Dr. Balaban (center) headed the branch in Warsaw,
Moshe Aron Reguer (front center), 1925

Part I

Europe

Lithuanian Jewish history begins with the general move of Jews from western and central Europe eastward. While the Crusades were a push factor for migration, a pull factor developed in the fifteenth century as the kings and nobles of Poland and Lithuania encouraged Jews to settle in their lands. They knew of the typically high education level of the Jews, of their skills, and of their trading ties.

Fifteenth-century Poland/Lithuania was feudal, with huge estates and a large peasant population. It needed managers for the estates, and people with business acumen for trade. A number of the region's new Jewish residents fit the bill, and by the end of the sixteenth century they had become managers for noblemen, as well as craftspeople, traders, and customs collectors.

These Jews, who were of the Ashkenazi tradition, brought with them the language that their people had developed in Germany and, since they lived separate from both native peasants and rulers and did not find themselves challenged intellectually by their new environment, Judeo-German, also known as Yiddish, remained their language. As with all Jewish languages, Yiddish is written in Hebrew characters.

Intellectual life was focused on traditional talmudic scholarship, and a variety of academies, *yeshivot*, were founded. The highest level of scholarship was reserved only for the most promising young men, but the majority of the Jews received basic education, and most men were literate. Education was part of communal structure, and there were thousands of Jewish communities, large and small, throughout the region. These communities were largely autonomous, and each provided its members with the necessities of Jewish life.

In a move that was unusual in diaspora Jewish history, the Jews of Eastern Europe set up a kind of Jewish parliament, the Council of the Four Lands, which regulated Jewish life in the region from the late sixteenth century to the early eighteenth century. It was a lay body with rabbinic representatives, and it functioned through a network of regional and local organizations.

The Jewish community of Brest-Litovsk, also called Brisk de-Lita, probably started in the fourteenth century and gradually became one of the main centers of Lithuanian Jewish life. Located on the Bug River, it was at a junction point of a number of commercial trade routes. The local Jews were involved in commerce, and traded in textiles and furs with Poland, Germany, and Austria. By the late fifteenth century the community also boasted commercial ties with Venice. As the Commonwealth of Poland/Lithuania (which also included the Baltic States and Belarus) came into being in 1569, Jews were heavily involved in crafts, tax-farming, and government jobs. The Jews had charters of protection, and Brest-Litovsk took a leading position in the communal and cultural affairs of the Council of the Four Lands.

When Hasidism came into existence in the eighteenth century, with its stress on prayer, piety, mysticism, and the role of the *Tzaddik*, or leader, the Jews of Brest-Litovsk took a leading role in fighting this new interpretation of Judaism, which they viewed as heterodox. These opponents of Hasidism were called *Mitnagdim* (pronounced in Yiddish as *Misnagdim*) and were led by Elijah of Vilna, known as the Gaon of Vilna (1720-1797).

Meanwhile, on the political stage, Brest-Litovsk, along with huge chunks of Eastern Europe, was incorporated into the expanding Russian Empire. Russia was expanding both into territories that had been under Ottoman Turkish control and westward into Poland, which was partitioned with Austria and Prussia. Russia—a strongly antisemitic nation—now found itself in control of a large population of Jews which it did not want to "pollute Holy Mother Russia." Thus was the Pale of Settlement born: Jews could only reside in the areas they were already in, and could not relocate to places like St. Petersburg.

When Nicholas I became Czar in 1825, a new solution for dealing with the Jews was found: a quota of Jewish boys to serve in the military was established. The term for military service was twenty-five years, starting at age eighteen, but Jewish boys were taken at age twelve for special units and were known as Cantonists, until they turned eighteen, when they went into the regular military units. During this time, great efforts were made to convert them to Russian Orthodox

Christianity. The Jewish communities called the recruiters *Khappers*, or "kidnappers," and, since community leaders were responsible for meeting the quotas, the system caused great antagonism within the Jewish world as well: the rich protected their own sons at the expense of the poor.

In 1881, Czar Alexander II was assassinated, and the Jews were blamed. A series of pogroms organized by the government took place in the Pale of Settlement. Western pressure led to a government investigation into the causes of the pogroms, an investigation which placed the blame squarely upon the Jews themselves. This then resulted in the May Laws of 1882, which, among other thing, expelled Jews from many villages and placed quotas on how many Jews could attend universities.

There is no doubt that these pogroms and antisemitic laws began the major demographic move from Eastern Europe to the Americas. The other major factor was the economic pull of the Americas, especially the religiously tolerant United States. For those Jews who remained, an attractive ideology was socialism in all its forms. For a very small group, Zionism was perceived as the solution to the Jews' problems.

Meanwhile, in Brest-Litovsk, the Russians threw down the Jewish quarter and in 1832 erected a fortress in its place. The government then built the Dnieper-Bug Canal in 1841, which led to the further growth of the city, including the erection of a tobacco factory, large mills, a hospital, and a new synagogue, despite the destruction of the old quarter.

The Jewish population of the city grew from over 8,000 people in the middle of the nineteenth century to over 30,000 by its end, making up seventy percent of the city's population. Then came World War I, and life changed.

The nineteenth century brought another change to Jewish Lithuania: a new structure to the yeshiva system, with its tradition of intensive study of the core texts of Jewish literature by elite, advanced students. This came about in part as a reaction to the challenges of modernization. The history of the Enlightenment is complex and is intimately connected with the philosophical and intellectual revolution that took place in Western Europe, which led to the secularization of society as well as to modern nationalism. Some Jews saw the benefits of modernity and wanted to spread the new ideas of the Enlightenment, known by the Jews as the Haskalah. Beginning in Germany with the writings of Moses Mendelssohn and his followers, the Haskalah reached the Jews of the Pale of Settlement through a complex route that involved writing about modern ideas in Hebrew, as most of the Eastern European students did not know German but were well versed in Hebrew. Hebrew textbooks and literature laid the groundwork for the language's revival. By the end of the nineteenth century, the same was true for Yiddish.

For traditionalists, modernization was more complex. They could not countenance overthrowing a system and society that was based on respecting authority and precedent. If change were to take place and succeed, it would have to come from within the traditional system.

The yeshiva system of Eastern Europe had a long history, and the schools were traditionally communal institutions. The new type of Lithuanian yeshiva, however, was independent of the community, and its economy was based on the collection of funds by traveling emissaries rather than on local community support. The new yeshivot were built in small towns rather than in big cities, and each *rosh yeshiva* or academic head ran his institution autonomously. This isolation from the local Jewish structure also encouraged strong student organization. Students were often dependent on the yeshiva for financial support as well, adding to the power of the *rosh yeshiva.*

A typical rosh yeshiva gave regular lectures, but most study was independent. The yeshiva was for unmarried teenage boys, and their building that was just for them and was not intended for any community purpose. Attendance was not compulsory, and acquiring rabbinical ordination was not a priority. There were also, generally, no regular examinations. The focus was on student discussion. Spiritual development was the concern of specially appointed supervisors or *mashgihim.*

Traditional yeshivot reacted in a variety of ways to the challenges of modernity. One way was to reform study methods, returning to earlier methods, and this was advocated by the Volozhin Yeshiva. A second was to reform social values through the study of ethics, or *musar,* and this was characteristic of the Slobodka Yeshiva. A third strategy was to reform the organization of education using such modern methods as dividing students into classes, having examinations, and setting up procedures for accepting students, and this was adopted by the Telz Yeshiva. The fourth, and most radical, method was used in Lida Yeshiva, and involved reforming the curriculum to include secular education.

My grandfather was a product of the Volozhin Yeshiva and spent most of his adult life in Brest-Litovsk. My father, born there, remained there until his teenage years, when he began his travels in search of a way to achieve his educational and intellectual goals. He studied for a while in the Telz Yeshiva and for a number of years in the Slobodka Yeshiva, both in Ukraine during World War I and back in Lithuania after the war.

Introduction/Preface to *My Memoirs*
(Written 25 Heshvan 1926)

About six months ago, an idea ignited in me to begin to write a "memoir of my childhood" that would open a window on my early daily life and would be a memento for the coming years. I began to feel the need for such a memento especially in the last few years. I left the stage of youth and entered the stage of young adulthood. My development has grown and widened. My world outlook is expanding. My life has become more nuanced, and my comprehension has grown until I am now able to analyze, more or less, various events and dreams. Because of all this, my life has become more important and relevant, so that it would be a shame if it passed and disappeared without a token or memory: it is a life that could be important for future years. So I decided to act on my thoughts.

Another important impetus—and it may be the most basic one—influenced me to follow up this idea. My life left the peace and tranquility of youth and became more agitated. I could not distance myself from the various winds that had begun to blow. The [Zionist] pioneer movement and the potential life of liberating labor in Eretz Israel have forced me to face a very difficult question. My life up to now, with its various yeshivas and afterwards the study of secular things, with perhaps a glowing future career, versus the lure of the pioneer Zionist movement, fought and are still doing battle within me. There is no peace for me. My heart is in a constant internal struggle, which rips me apart with its flames. I think that my memoirs will serve me well, giving me the opportunity to think through my ideas and my emotions. I was to have begun this at the start of the summer, but I pushed it off until after the holidays for a variety of personal reasons. Since I want the memoirs to be complete, to shed light on my development, I will attempt to do my best to record the details of what happened to me from my birth until now.

Q. What year were you born — what is written on your passport?

A. November 20, 1905. **[He was in fact born in 1903; the passport stated 1905 for reasons that will be discussed — Ed.]**

Q. In what city?

A. Brest-Litovsk

Q. Where is that?

A. Now it belongs to Russia. **[While this was the case at the time of this interview, now it is in Belarus — Ed.]**

Q. To whom did it belong in 1905?

A. Also Russia, but under the Tsar.

Q. What were the names of your parents?

A. Rav Simcha Zelig and Sorke.

Q. How many brothers and sisters did you have?

A. I had two brothers and four sisters: Chaim, the oldest, Shimon, Feigl, Golde, Esther, and Peshke.

So began the first official interview of my father, when he was seventy-three years old; the second was four years later. He had always told me stories of his life, and when I was small they seemed like children's stories. As a product of a Lithuanian yeshiva education, he truly did not know fairy tales. When my mother told him to put me to bed and I demanded my story, however, she wouldn't take over. Instead she told him, "Tell her what you know." In this way I learned gory and exciting legends of the Jews, in addition to the tales of my father's youth. As I grew older, I saw my father sitting at the dining room table with his Talmud or with other Judaica, studying and crying. The American attitude that "men didn't cry," was not part of my experience, for I observed that when the *yahrzeit* of my father's parents arrived, and he learned a set of *mishnayot* in their honor, he always cried over his losses. It was not long after I achieved realization that my father began to tell me stories of his mother and father and granted me a self-censored slew of family lore. I say self-censored because he kept in mind that I was a little girl and would not understand things like Nazi brutality, Communism, Zionism, Bolshevism, Freudian relationships, and hubris, to name a few. That understanding came gradually over the years.

But I could never get him to sit down in front of a tape recorder. What the reader cannot hear through these written transcripts, of course, is the intonation of the words. For example, the laughter accompanying the first question—"What year were you born—on your passport?" We all knew that my father was not born in 1905 but in 1903. His documents, however, dating back to his visa to Mandatory Palestine in 1926, listed 1905 probably in order to ease his way out of Poland, which was drafting young men who were not students into the army. A twenty-three-year-old would have raised suspicions, as the assumption would be that his education was complete; a twenty-one-year-old could easily be assumed to be a student.

Q. Tell me about your mother. Who was your mother?

A. In Brisk my mother was called Sorke Reb Simcha Zelig's because Simcha Zelig was the Rosh Av Bet Din in Brisk, and there were other women named Sorke.

Q. What was your mother's background?

A. She was born in Volozhin to Rav Avraham Yaakov Yoykhens and Rotke [Rudensky].

Q. She was the oldest? The middle?

A. She was the oldest and had two sisters. [**She also had three brothers—Ed.**]

Q. What about your grandmother and grandfather? What did your grandmother look like?

A. Rotke was well known in all of Volozhin because she supported her husband—he studied Talmud and made *siyyums* on all of *Shas*. They lived in Volozhin the whole time. Rotke used to sell whiskey to the Gentiles who would come several times a week from the villages. She knew how to deal with them—she spoke Russian well, as well as Polish, and they had great respect for her. It was a whiskey store and the house was at the side. The store was big, and there were tables. And she was the only one who could control them because they respected her so much.

Q. Did they have anyone else helping or did she do it all herself?

A. When a niece grew up—Rav Yoykhens's daughter Feigl—she helped her. [**This was the daughter of Sorke's brother Yochanan Rudensky—Ed.**]

Q. How did she get the store to start with? Did she rent it? Buy it?

A. I don't know.

Q. Do you know anything about Rotke's parents?

A. No.

Q. Did you ever visit them in Volozhin?

A. During the First World War we were forced out of Brisk. Father and Reb Haim [Soloveitchik] traveled to Minsk and we continued on to Volozhin.

Q. How long were you in Volozhin?

A. A year. Until we could go back to Brisk. We suffered from Feigl's awful attitude.

Q. How many of you went?

A. The whole family. My brothers were not in Poland.

Q. What about your grandfather Reb Avraham Yankl?

A. He was quite a type, which you don't see often even in Volozhin. There were two Avraham Yankls, so to differentiate, they added the third generation, Yoykhn, to the name. He would *daven* [leading the service] on Yom Kippur because the Netziv [**acronym for Rav Naftali Zvi Yehuda Berlin, Rosh Yeshiva from 1853—Ed.**] asked him to. He was originally from Volozhin. He was a very good-looking man with a nice beard and very clean, because Rotke was very strict about cleanliness.

Q. What did she look like?

A. He was a little taller than her. She was some personality and it showed in her face, in her voice, in her actions— in everything. I have very seldom found such a woman.

Q. This is your mother's side of the family, and they were Volozhiners. Your grandfather had the responsibility of marrying off his three daughters. How did he find a husband for your mother?

A. The Netziv told my grandfather that even though there were 500 students in the yeshiva, he felt that there was no one suitable to be my *Zayde's* son-in-law. This is what he told me.

Q. Was your grandfather so special?

A. Yes. The Netziv said that there was a *meshulach*
(emissary)—the same one who had brought the
Meitchiter Illui [**Shlomo Polachek of Maitchet—Ed.**]
to him as a child of seven—who had just come to tell the
Netziv that during a visit to the small town of Ilya, close
to Vilna, he had met a young man who was a *Baki* in *Shas*
and *Yerushalmi*, a *Masmid*, who knew more than any other
young man he had met. [**Volozhin Yeshiva was the first
yeshiva to become independent of community support.
It did this by sending emissaries out to collect funds.
This gave the yeshiva autonomy, and the rosh yeshiva
great authority.** *Baki* **was a colloquial term for someone
extraordinarily knowledgeable—Ed.**]

Q. What did your grandfather do as a result of that?

A. He immediately took my mother Sorke and went to meet
with my father in Ilya.

Q. The marriages were arranged, but the woman had to
agree?

A. They had to see each other—just to make a wedding
without seeing or meeting? Never. It just happened
that the floor of the inn was of earth and uneven and
my father sat where it was low and my mother cried all
night thinking that he was very short. [**The fact was that
she was very short herself and probably had images of
midget-size children—Ed.**] In fact he was much taller

than she was. My mother was twenty-three and my father was twenty, and they informed him of this [age difference].

Q. How about your father's parents?

A. My father's mother was named Peshe and his father was named Reb Dov, and they lived in Navaradok and he was a teacher of Talmud. And this is what my father told me — don't laugh — because he was a very weak child my *Zayde* and *Bobbe* bought a goat and they would milk the goat and give him the milk so that he would be stronger. There was once a storm and the goat was killed and because of this they left Navorodok and came to Brisk. My *Zayde* immediately found work in a Talmud Torah. Rav Yosef Dov Soloveitchik [Yoshe Ber] — the author of the *Beit Levi* — tested my father, who was only seven. He said that my father would be a *gadol be-yisrael* (a major scholar).

Q. Do you know the year your father was born? Can you approximate?

A. No. I can't. [**Research shows that this was likely around 1863 — Ed.**]

Q. So how did he get from Brisk to Ilya?

A. His father could not support him — how much did a melamed make? — and he had a brother, Rav Alter, and a sister too — so he went to Ilya because we had these relatives. In Ilya he sat and studied day and night and he "ate days" [**ate at the tables of various rich**

patrons—Ed.]. So he told me. In Ilya, he was sitting on
the same seat that Graf Pototsky had sat on while he was
hiding from the Polish government before they killed him.
**[Walentyn Potocki, d. 1749, was killed for converting
to Judaism—Ed.]**

Q. Until he was twenty?

A. Yes.

Q. Where did the wedding take place?

A. In Volozhin. And at the time, the Netziv took him to be
one of the first "Brodetskys'" (scholarship recipients)—
the rich man Brodetsky from Moscow had given money,
four rubles a month, for young married men to sit and
learn and support a family. Four rubles was a lot. He had
the four rubles until the end of his life, and on the *yahrzeit*
he used to study all the *mishnayot* for Brodetsky—for his
Jewish name—and the day of the *yahrzeit* he was busy
all day. [**The name of the man was Yisrael Brodsky,
and his family, which became wealthy through sugar
production, was from Kiev. The family set up a Kollel
for married men to study Jewish law and codes. The
selection was made by the Volozhin Yeshiva—Ed.**]

Q. Where did they live?

A. In Volozhin. Who recommended that he be a "Brodetsky"?
The Netziv, for he thought very highly of Father.
And there Father connected strongly with Rav Haim
Soloveitchik. When Rav Yoshe Ber lost the *Din Torah* with

Rav Yitzchak Elchanan and was dismissed from being
a Rosh Yeshiva, the Netziv became the Rosh Yeshiva of
Volozhin, and [my father] met Rav Haim through the
Netziv. And from the moment R Haim met my father, he
did not let go of him—he was much older, but "his hand
did not move from his hand"—it is not an exaggeration.
So when R Yoshe Ber died in Brisk and they wanted him
as Rav, R Haim said only on condition that they invite
Father, too, from Volozhin. And so it was. They waited
until father came from Volozhin and he was made *Rosh
Av Bet Din*. He told me that in the meantime, before Rav
Haim demanded that he come to Brisk, he was looking
for a *rabbanut*. He found out that in Porets, near Bobruisk,
there was a vacancy where they were looking for a Rav.
So he came and he spoke in *halakha* and in *aggada*, and
after Shabbat they told him openly that the *halakha* we
like, but you are not a good speaker. Therefore they
refused him the *rabbanut*. Later on, when Father became
famous, they were ashamed. It was the same year that
they closed Volozhin Yeshiva (on January 22, 1892). In
those days the yeshiva was closed because one of the
students *massered* (informed) and wrote a letter signing
the name of the Netziv, and in a second letter he wrote
that the Netziv is a spy and all the students are spies in
Volozhin and the reason why he sent this is because—
Father told me—when he came in on Yom Kippur, the

Netziv recognized that he had eaten, which was true, and he came over and gave him a slap in the face in the presence of everybody. And this he couldn't stand and therefore he *massered* on the yeshiva and they sent soldiers from Vilna and they surrounded the yeshiva and they asked, "Where is the Netziv?" And they showed the Netziv the letter, and asked if it was his signature, and he said, "Yes, it is my signature." But at the trial in Vilna he recognized that this was a forgery because in all of his letters, after he wrote "Netziv," he never made a dot and this was with a dot. And they believed him and he was free, but they officially closed the Yeshiva. [**This is one variant. In chapter 8 of Shaul Stampfer's** *Lithuanian Yeshivas of the Nineteenth Century*,* **Stampfer concludes that the Russian authorities were concerned with order, and the unrest of the students in Volozhin at that time worried them—Ed.**]

In the early years of my grandfather's life in Brisk, there occurred an episode that became almost legendary in the city. It seems that there was a billy goat which was uncontrollable. He ran wild in the city, pulling down hanging laundry, eating whatever he could, knocking down children, and in general becoming

---

* Shaul Stampfer, *Lithuanian Yeshivas of the Nineteenth Century* (Oxford: The Littman Library of Jewish Civilization, 2012).

a danger to the community. However, due to the Jewish tradition of not harming first-born animals, which were sacred to God and in biblical times would have been brought to the Temple for the priests, the Jews could not touch the goat.

"Rabbi, what can we do? The beast is endangering our children and our old people," an unofficial committee said to Rabbi Simcha Zelig. My grandfather thought a bit, probably stroking his long white beard, for so my father described his usual thinking position, and responded:

"You know that the exception to the rule of the sanctity of a first born animal is if there is a *moom*, a blemish, on his body."

"But Rabbi, I thought that we can't touch him!"

"You can't. However, he can have an accident...."

So that is how the entire Jewish community of Brisk went on a goat hunt. They chased the wicked billy goat down the alleys, blocking his path, until he jumped up onto one of the lowhanging rooftops, which he was known for doing. But this time some of the men and boys jumped up after him, and everyone was yelling. The goat became disoriented, leaped off the roof in his attempt to reach another rooftop, and missed. He fell hard on his shoulder, and without any further ado, the *shokhet*—ritual slaughterer—who had been chasing along with the crowd until then stepped forward while a number of strong men held the goat down, and proceeded to slaughter the animal, to the cheers of the crowd.

Q. By the time your father and mother moved to Brisk, how
many children were there?

A. Two children had died in Volozhin. Haim was the only
one born in Volozhin [who survived].

My father had family pictures to illustrate his stories. As
a child, I did not really understand ages. An adult man was an
adult man. But one day it dawned on me to ask if my grandfather
had always been old. My father saw that I was looking at
a photograph of a fairly young Simcha Zelig, but that his hair and
beard were all white. So he told me a story.

The first child that Sorke and Simcha Zelig had was a boy.
The great excitement over a first-born male was felt by all, and
he was duly named and began to take his place in the family.
But then tragedy struck the young couple: the child caught one
of the many childhood diseases rampant in Eastern Europe and
died of diphtheria. My grandfather's hair and beard turned white
overnight, and people referred to this by quoting the Talmud,
saying that "it was like he was seventy years old" [in a reference
to the talmudic figure Rabbi Eliezer, who was said to have gone
white overnight at a young age].

When my mother heard my crying over this sad tale, she
came running into the room, berating my father for upsetting
me with one of his stories. But I said that I was a big girl and
could hear bad things too. Little did I know what was in store
for me.

Q. What did the community provide for your father?

A. He was the Chief Justice and Rosh Yeshiva of "Mishmar Beis Medrash," and he taught. Among his students was Rav Unterman, who later became Chief Rabbi of Tel Aviv, who got *semicha* from Father.

Q. Who bought the house?

A. The house did not belong to us but to the community. It had two floors. We lived above Rav Haim and his wife Livshe. One could just pop into the Soloveitchiks' home via the stairs. If he needed Father, [R. Haim] would just go up the stairs or the other way around. There was also a courtyard.

My father told me that he and R Haim were distant relatives: Rav Haim Brisker descended from Rav Haim Volozhener, who had two brothers—the elder brother was Rav Simcha and the younger was Rav Zalman, who died very young. And Father was named "Simcha Zelig" after R Simcha; they added the "Zelig" when he was sick. We are descended from Rav Simcha, Rav Haim Volozhener's brother. He was a *Gaon Olam*. The world knows about Rav Haim because he founded the yeshiva and was the Vilna Gaon's most outstanding student, but both brothers were *Geonim*.

From the time I was little, my father kept telling me the importance of *yichus* or lineage. Why is this important? I asked.

Because it marks you off as a leader, and the probable parent of probably brilliant children, he would answer. I did not pay much attention to this until I was an adult. However, my father kept harping on the actual list of names, so I memorized them just to make him happy. We started with Rav Yitzhak (who had no last name because there were very few Ashkenazi Jews with last names during his time) who was the father of Ha-Rav ha-Gaon Simcha and his younger brother Ha-Rav Chaim of Volozhin. Simcha was the father of a nameless daughter, who married Rav Yosef. (Why is she nameless? I asked. Because women were not as important as men then. But isn't she the direct descendant? Yes. So? So.) She had a nameless daughter herself, who married Rav Sha'ul, who was the father of a nameless daughter who married Rav Zvi-Hirsh, who was the father of Esther. (So we know her name? Yes, probably because my father remembered her personally.) Esther married Rav Shimon of Navorodok, and was the mother of Rav Dov (Berl) who was the father of Simcha Zelig, my grandfather.

Rav Dov's last name was Mogilensky, and he lived at the time of the *Khappers*, the Kidnappers. These were the feared members of the Russian army who came to grab little Jewish boys and draft them for twenty-five years of military service for the Tsar. Two of the very few ways to save one's sons from this horrible possibility was to bribe the Russians or to have only one son—single sons were exempt from service. Rav Dov, father of three sons, Alter, Simcha Zelig, and Shlomo Chaim, gave each one a different last name, and when the Russians came to the town where he lived, he said that the other two were single sons of cousins living in the countryside who were staying with him in order to receive an education. That is how my grandfather got the surname Reguer (var. Riger, Rijer, Rieger, Ryjer). He carried that name long enough for him to decide not to go back to the original one in later decades, after the fall of the Tsarist government.

A footnote to all of this is that Rabbi Yitzhak Elchanan Spektor, also of Navorodok, was my grandfather's *sandek* (similar to a godfather) at his *brit mila*, his circumcision.

In the yeshiva world all of these details are important, and it constantly astonishes me how many people memorize all of these lineages.

Q. So you were born in that house?

A. Yes, not in a hospital.

Q. Who were you named after?

A. In Brisk, there was a nephew of my father [**his sister's son—Ed.**] who was a *dayan*; his name was Moshe Aron, and he was childless. He went to Eretz Israel—he was exceptional in learning and also invented a machine which could measure the water in the *miqve*— how much was natural and how much was not (*mayim shiurim*). He was superb in practical application of learning. When he died, the news arrived, and, at my circumcision, when the *sandek* heard the name which I was given, he cried because he had known

R Moshe Aron and was sad that he had died in Eretz
Israel.

Q. You were the sixth of seven children. Do you remember
the birth of your little sister?

A. No.

**My father had six siblings who reached adulthood: Uncle
Chaim, Uncle Shimon, Aunt Feigl, Aunt Esther, Aunt Goldie, and
Aunt Peshke. There were more than twenty-five years between the
eldest and the youngest siblings, which means that generational
differences appeared often in my father's stories. Of course it took
me years to realize this.**

*The city of my birth is Brisk de-Lita, Grodna province.
My birthday was not recorded in a book, because this was
not done then by our people. I was told that I was born
25 Heshvan 1903 (5662). My father, the Gaon Rav Simcha
Zelig ... of Brisk, is very respected in the entire world of [yeshiva]
scholarship and specifically in my city and its surroundings,
for the depth and breadth of his legal knowledge, his "derekh
eretz," and his proper behavior. His twenty-four-hour day was
divided into one third for study and teaching others for free,
one third for legal decisions, and one third for himself—for his
needs and for the public. And I was the beloved son; he chose
me over his other sons to educate me in the ways of God. When
I was six years old, and already knew how to read, he turned*

me over to one of the best teachers in our city to teach me Torah
with the proper translations and commentaries. This teacher
was Reb Nachum from Slonim, who worked meticulously
twelve hours a day. After three years I knew almost the whole
Tanakh by heart and God's Torah was indelibly inscribed
in me.

Q. Would you describe your education?

A. In Brisk I learned. At seven I learned *gemara* with Rav
   Zeltzer. He was a very good rebbe.

Q. How many children did you learn with?

A. At least ten—in the *rebbe's* house. In the big room, half
   was for teaching us and the other half, divided by
   a curtain, had beds. He had unbelievable patience—
   a lively man.

Q. Did you *daven* (say the daily morning, afternoon, and
   evening services) in class or at home?

A. In Brisk we *davened* in *shul*, and then we ate something
   in the house and then went to learn until night. On
   Chanuka, I had to carry a special Chanuka lamp
   at night.

Q. Did you take food from home? Did the *rebbe's* wife feed
   you?

A. I don't remember. This was a side issue. The only
   important thing was learning.

Q. And you sat until it was *maariv* time?

A. Yes. Once we put on the play "Yosef and his Brothers."
We did this in *shul*. And the *rebbe* was very *frum*
(stringent) but he allowed it. I remember until today
how the boy playing Yosef was outstanding. It was so
nice. It was the first theater in my life. *Chumash*
I learned with Father. He knew the entire *Tanakh*
the way an ordinary Jews knows *"Ashrei"*
(a basic prayer taught to children). Then I started
gemara and I learned until we had to go away because
of the war.

Q. Until the war, when you were having this wonderful
education, what was happening with your younger sister
Peshke?

A. She also learned, like the other two sisters. But there
wasn't a *cheder* for girls.

Q. So did your father teach her like he did you?

A. He taught her, but not on the same level as me. What
a question! She knew *chumash*, reading, writing. She
had a good head on her shoulders.

Q. And when you sat around the table Friday night?

A. We used to talk and sing.

Q. Everyone? Who served?

A. It depended. After my sister Feigl got married, she used
to bring the food since it was hard for Mother to do
everything. There was a time when we had a woman
helping.

Q. When you built your *succa* [**a small outdoor hut used for the holiday of *Succos* in the autumn — Ed.**] — did you share it with Rav Haim? Or did you have your own?

A. We had ours upstairs. Father opened a wing and there was the *succa*. When Father made a *hupa* (a wedding ceremony), he used to open it too.

Q. So people would just come to get married in front of the rabbi? What about a party?

A. What kind of business? They paid *groschen*. [**Pennies. In other words, they would not make a party — Ed.**]

Q. When you were sitting in the succa, did the women sit too?

A. Everybody!

Q. And all *bentched lulav* and *esrog* (performed the ritual blessing over the Four Species on the holiday)?

A. What kind of question? Everyone did. Father made sure that you *bentched* — he would keep asking, "Did you *bentch*?" And it was taken for granted!

My father described the house as having two large bedrooms, one tiny one, a kitchen, and a large central room that was used as a dining room/study. The kitchen held the wood-burning stove, the cooking utensils, cutlery, basins of all sizes, and a tub for laundry and bathing. There was no indoor plumbing and no indoor toilet. The town's Jews finally paid for indoor plumbing just as World War II began, just before the Nazis occupied the house.

When all of the girls lived at home, the second bedroom was occupied by them. The two older sons were long out of the house, living first at yeshivas and then on their own. But things changed as the girls grew up. Meanwhile, my grandmother had to do all of the cooking, cleaning, laundry, and child-care herself. Life was not easy.

My grandfather's custom was not to visit cemeteries. You buried the dead, you marked the *yahrzeit* by studying *mishnayot*, one chapter for each letter of the deceased's name, matching the chapter's initial letter to the letter of the name. Even the custom of visiting cemeteries during the month of Elul, which is followed by the majority of Jews the world over, was not to my grandfather's liking. My grandmother, by contrast, went to the cemetery often. She went to visit the graves of her dead first-born and all of her other babies who had died during childbirth or soon thereafter. My father said that my grandmother gave birth at least thirteen times. She went to the cemetery to cry, and my grandfather understood this, and understood how hard her life was, so he looked the other way instead of imposing his views on his wife. His compassion for others was part of his international reputation, for in his *halakhic* decisions, he was a *meikil*, a decisor who searched for the least onerous legal decision. It was very easy to say no, and to see Judaism as black or white, but that is not the true Jewish way—it is in the gray areas that we must function.

It is ironic that this was my grandfather's way, since no one knows where he is buried and therefore no one can ever visit his

grave. In effect, we are forced to observe his custom in regard to him.

When I was nine, my father turned me over to the Talmud teacher Reb Yitzhok from Seltz. He took me to the threshold of the enormous ancient Talmud, the "Og king of Bashan" in the literature of the world. When I came [to the border], I was like a man who came for the first time to the big market day, gazing in wonder at all of the varied goods and wares, incredulous at the noise coming from all sides. Buyers and sellers noisily looking and selling, rushing here and there, this one with his sack, that one with his cart, pushing, shouting, haggling, weighing. With my ability to visualize things, I imagined the shapes and faces of the Talmud. The Tana Kama, and "hai man de-amar" seemed to me like men easily aroused and their faces were alive; the Reisha, Seifa, Metsiatah were like competing women, each one rivaling the other, this one saying yes and this one saying no, and they were angry and unsettled; and here the deaf, the fool, the minor, the "zav," the "zava," and the two holding the "tallit"; here was the ox that gored the cow, the holiday ox, and the ox of the fool—and all came alive in my imagination, each as an individual. I understood the language of each as I met them because from my childhood I had acquired the language of the Targumim (i.e. Aramaic), but much of their conversation I did not understand properly. But that was just at the beginning, as I entered the gate of the

Talmud: with time I became comfortable with it and loved it deeply. I rested on the depths of the law. **[Following is a list of topics studied, redacted in this translation—Ed.]**

At the age of ten I left my teacher's cheder because the Great War broke out and all of the residents of my city were expelled. My entire family left and went as refugees to the city of Volozhin, Vilna province, to my mother's father, the great rabbi Avraham Rudensky.

Q. Who took care of you when you were a child?
A. My sisters. My mother was too busy. She had no help.
   Father used to earn very little—he was not one of those people who made money. He didn't know what money was.

My father told me numerous stories about his sisters. The three older ones played very important roles in his life, and it seemed that they raised him more than his mother did. Perhaps the reason it seemed that way is that over the years my grandmother must have delegated various jobs to the girls. They helped in the kitchen, they helped dress him, and they played with him, as much as he did play, considering that he started going to school full-time at the age of three. When he began school, he had the typical first-day-of-class experience of Eastern European Jewish boys: the fuss, the new clothes, and the letters written in honey

to teach him that the experience of learning Hebrew would be a sweet one. Little did his family members know as they celebrated just how important the study of this language, in both its biblical and its modern forms, would become in my father's life.

Q. Where did you get food?

A. [My father] used to answer all legal questions—of the lungs, gasot, *dakot*—so the butchers used to pay him in kind, with meat, because they didn't have the money to pay. And we always ate meat for Shabbat.

Q. What did you eat during the week?

A. All kind of things.

Q. Did your sisters work?

A. Later my sisters became nurses in the hospital. Father allowed them to work on Shabbat.

Q. Did they have to get an education to be a nurse?

A. They had an education. Father was not against this. They took four years of classes. Golde and Esther supplemented the family's income.

Q. Your oldest sister was already married?

A. Yes, when we were refugees.

Q. Tell me about your *seders*.

A. Father used to stop on every word and every small thing while we read the *Haggada*, and explained every minute detail. Once when he was explaining a section, he began to cry over the *tzarot* that we had in Egypt. Another time, when I was really small, I was fighting with my sister Peshke under the table. I hit her so much that she started crying and yelling. Then Father hit me. I can never forget it, for Mother begged him to stop. Stop! He can die from such slaps!, she said. Father was far from anxious to hit anyone. He never hit the children, especially not me. But this was too much. But I was a child! What did I know?

Q. So you all sat and discussed and he explained everything.

A. Yes. He had *shmura* matza, but only for him, for you needed teeth of iron for it. But he ate it. He was strict not to eat anything else, but he allowed us to.

Q. He was a *meikil* for everyone except himself?

A. On everything. For example, Saturday night, after *maariv*, he waited seventy-two minutes according to Rabeinu Tam [before he would consider Shabbat to have ended]. He asked everyone else not to wait, but they waited.

One of the Responsa that my grandfather was famous for was the question of the International Dateline. If a person was on a ship traveling east from Japan and it was Yom Kippur, when he crossed the International Dateline, did he have to fast a second day since it was Yom Kippur on that side of the line? This was one of the only times in his career that my grandfather made a *makhmir* decision, for he was known for being a *maykil*. He said that the person had to fast two days.

On the *maykil* side, he followed the custom of not having a bride and groom fast on the day of their wedding. He felt that they were nervous enough as it was; it was inhumane, therefore, to expect them to fast as well. He was not a big advocate of fasting other than on Yom Kippur and on Tisha B'Av anyway.

Father had twenty decisions (psakim) that are not recorded in the books of Rav Haim. And these twenty decisions are in the Beit ha-Rav in America and in Israel. I asked Rav Soloveitchik's son if he could give them to me. So far I have not received them. He said he had asked his father, who had agreed.

My father told me that before my grandmother got sick, one of the things that she took upon herself to do was to feed all of the poor Jews on the eve of Pesach. During the interval between getting rid of the *chametz* and sitting down at the *seder* with the festive meal, it was almost impossible for poor Jews to find anything to eat. So, for lunch on that day my grandmother prepared huge pots of borscht, which could be eaten with potatoes. She and her three older daughters would peel mountains of beets and cook them in the traditional Jewish way, that is, without meat, and serve it piping hot to the line of poor people waiting outside the door of the house. This traditional act of *hesed* added to her positive reputation as the wife of the chief *dayyan*.

The Volozhin Chapter

I came to Volozhin when I was ten. Volozhin is one of the most praised cities in the yeshiva world. As a result of my parents' fear that I would forget my Torah learning, I was sent to the yeshiva "bochur" Mordekhai Isser Taub of Bialistok. I studied with him one hour a day at the cost of four rubles a month. My parents left Volozhin and returned to Brisk, and because I did not want to remain alone they listened to my request and left my sister [Feigl] with me. We rented a flat, but for Shabbatot we ate at my grandfather's (Rav Avraham's) table—he who was constantly immersed in Torah. The location of my classes with Mordekhai Isser was in the yeshiva. On my visits there, I entered into discussions with the young students, and from them I learned that in the city there was a school with four levels, and the language used was Russian. Without knowing why, though now I feel it was partly because of envy of others and partly to make up for my lack of [secular] education, one day—without consulting my sister—I went to the director of the school and was accepted to the first level. There I studied the Russian alphabet—reading and writing. After two days of intense work, I was put into the second level.

I went to this school in secret because I feared the reaction of my pious grandfather, who would surely have punished me had he known. My sister Feigl found out, but she could not stand up to me. She worried deep in her heart. So time passed, and then Satan came to interfere. One day, as I was returning from the school escorted by my friends, my cousin [a woman or girl, probably the one who was named Feigl—Ed.] *saw me. She understood what this meant and told my grandmother. She was furious and spilled her venom on my sister's head, and when I returned home the next day, my sister began to cry and begged me to stop studying secular subjects. I was forced to do so. My teachers sent one messenger after another, asking me to return and promising to promote me to the third level, but I was ashamed and did not return. This event made a strong impression on me and left a shadow lasting until today. That day I decided to forget about [secular] school, and I devoted myself to gemara.*

I went more often to the yeshiva and took more of an interest in it. At that time the excellent students were testing the younger ones—they were in the library in the yeshiva's basement. Their goal was to instill envy among the younger yeshiva students, for the best would receive a "very good grade;" and the others a "good"—they believed that "envy of writers will result in wisdom." During the exams, I answered the most difficult questions without too much thinking, and received a certificate with the grade "very good."

In those days a strange event occurred in the yeshiva. A famous young man arrived, Yonah ben Rav Malkiel [Tenenbaum] from Lomze. He was a tall young man with a large head and a pale face; he was known to have unusually deep knowledge and understanding. He made a strong impression on the yeshiva because he was a "Maskil" (Enlightened person, follower of the Haskalah) who had completed eight levels of schooling and received a certificate of matriculation. Rumor had it that he was a revolutionary who had participated in the 1905 event. As an "enlightened" person, he greatly influenced the yeshiva students, and a large group of them took Russian classes with him.

Sometimes I came to my teacher Mordekhai Isser's house and, in a second room, would meet a young man named Srulovitz. Often when I entered, I saw him bareheaded, writing in Russian and reading books that I understood to be secular. This made a huge impression on a boy of eleven, educated in a fundamentalist environment. I saw that there were also yeshiva students like this in the world, who dared to remove their hats without fear. I also saw my teacher and his yeshiva friends when they were preparing their Russian classes for Yonah of Lomze, and I understood that it was not so awful to break down the wall a bit and go outside....

That summer, my teacher Mordekhai Isser went to Vilna and handed me over to another student, Chaim, son of the rav of Smititz. It was said that he was going to Vilna for a marriage arrangement, but afterwards I was told that he had not traveled for that but to take the examination for the fourth level in our school—but he did not pass. Chaim, son of the rav of Smititz, was a happy and joyful lad. Often when I would go to him to study, I would find him with his brother Simcha, an excellent writer, who was bareheaded while playing the violin, singing, and dancing. The two brothers were always happy and lovers of life. They enlivened the yeshiva, especially on Simchat Torah. Then they would turn the world upside down and introduce a breath of fresh air into the dark, morbidly depressing walls of the yeshiva. Of one event of those days I have a clear memory: when I came to the house of my new teacher Chaim, I found many young men, among them Yonah of Lomze, discussing going for a walk. It was my luck to be liked by them, and they invited me too to participate in the walk. We left the city and came to "Bialik's mountain." (This is a mountain below a village where Bialik the poet, when studying in Volozhin yeshiva, used to walk and compose his poetry; even today there are to be found there the two big rocks upon which he sat while composing his poems.) The whole area there is naturally beautiful—Bialik knew what he was doing in choosing to write there—and from there we walked to the woods which were two parsangs* away. There Yonah met his beloved, the daughter of the rav from the valley

---

* About seven and a half miles; the Parsang was a Persian unit of measure.

of Volozhin. She was a smart and educated young woman, already a university student. Yonah walked with her, arm in arm. This was my first vision of romantic love, and it made a strong impression on me. In the village we drank milk (some bareheaded—that also influenced me) and we went to the forest. In the woods we sang and danced happily, and we returned towards evening to the city.

This one incident in particular from my life at the yeshiva remains in my heart as one of the important events of my life.

Volozhin Yeshiva was not like other yeshivas at that time.

Volozhin Yeshiva, formally known as "Etz Hayyim," was founded in 1803 by Rav Haim of Volozhin in part to prevent protect against inroads of Haskalah ideology, and, on a lesser level, to prevent inroads of Hasidism into the Lithuanian Jewish communities. It rapidly grew and became a prototype for later yeshivot. The school is considered to have raised the religious intellectual scholarship of Lithuanian Jewry above that of other contemporary yeshivas and high standards were set, through a reform of study methods in which analysis of the text was stressed. After Rav Haim's death in 1821, his son Rav Yitzhak became the rosh yeshiva, but since he was occupied with administration and financial affairs, the teaching was delegated to his two sons-in-law, Rav Eliezer Isaac Fried and Rav Naftali Zvi Yehuda Berlin, also known as the Netziv, who was mentioned

earlier. Rav Yitzhak died in 1848 and Rav Eliezer Isaac in 1854. This left the Netziv and Rav Joseph Ber Soloveitchik (R. Haim's grandson) as co-roshei yeshiva. The two had a major disagreement over control over various aspects of the yeshiva, and there is no doubt that it was personal as well. Although a delegation of leading Lithuanian rabbis settled the controversy, Rav Joseph Ber left in 1865 to become Rav of Brest-Litovsk. Rav Raphael Shapira, son-in-law of the Netziv, took his place, serving until 1881 when Rav Haim Soloveitchik, the son of Rav Joseph Ber, succeeded him.

In 1887, as a result of outside pressure, the yeshiva was supposed to introduce lessons in Russian and mathematics, but it did not. It could not, however, totally exclude the external influences of the *musar* movement, the Haskalah, and Zionism. In 1891, the Russian minister of education demanded that the school's pupils study basic general subjects. The Netziv refused, and in 1892 the yeshiva was closed. It reopened officially as a place of prayer in 1895, and beginning in 1899 it was run by Rav Raphael Shapira. It remained a functioning yeshiva until World War I interfered, with the battle zone reaching Vilna/Volozhin. Everyone headed further into Russia, to Minsk, and the school did not resume activity until 1921. It lasted, in this new form, until the Holocaust. Its last roshei yeshiva were Rav Yaakov Shapira (d. 1936) and his son-in-law Rav Hayyim Walkin.

The daily schedule—which served as a prototype for many other yeshivot—started with prayers at 8 a.m., followed by breakfast. Then part of the weekly Torah portion was read and explained by the rosh yeshiva prior to intense Talmud study lasting until 1 p.m., which was the time of the rosh yeshiva's lecture. After the lecture would be lunch and rest until 4 p.m., afternoon prayers, and then more study until 10 p.m., when night prayers were held, and then supper served at last. Many students followed this up by studying until midnight; for others, study resumed at 3 a.m.

This was a world of men, supported by an international network of fundraising. Teachers received regular salaries, and the students received stipends. Its graduates were even placed in jobs by the school.

There were no "rosh yeshiva" classes, and there was no unified curriculum. The students learned various "masekhtot" and these weren't even in one location—some studied in their dormitories, others in the bet midrash—and they came to the yeshiva only for in-depth discussions of various topics that often had nothing to do with gemara. Yet there were some "matmidim" who sat all day at the yeshiva. The rosh yeshiva at that time was Rav Raphael [Shapira] zl (of blessed memory), but because of his old age and weakness, he could not teach. On holidays he would summon the students to his house and there would give a class on his new ideas. When the war broke out, his son, Rav Yaakov [Shapira], an accomplished scholar, came to him as a refugee. He and the mashgiach, Rav Avraham Drushkovitz, wanted to appoint him rosh yeshiva in place of his father Rav Raphael. But this wish was strongly opposed by the yeshiva students, especially by those who loved Haskalah; they did not want a strong leader who would end their freedom. And so a huge dispute erupted between the yeshiva students on one side, and Rav Yaakov and his followers the "Brodoskaim" on the other. The most outstanding of the former group was Moshe Reuven, my future brother-in-law, who was an interesting type, and this became clear during the dispute with Rav Mordeshkovits (Drushkovitz?). He was different in his looks **[this mysterious comment is never explained—Ed.]** and especially his behavior. For example, I remember that he would eat only once a day, but during that meal he would eat a litre of meat at one time. Although he was generally strict, in this instance he sided with Rav Yaakov, and one time [the Rosh Yeshiva] became angry with Moshe Reuven for doing so, arose, grabbed him by the shoulder, and threw him out.

I too took part in the dispute. Once the opposition students gathered to meet in the library, which was located in the first floor of the building. I worked then allocating paper and writing instruments, and it was my task to gather the students for the meeting and to record those attending. I went to fetch Yitzhak of Melnik, who boarded at the home of a woman who was famous for her knowledge of Talmud and Hebrew, and who served as advisor to all. Rav Yitzhak Avigdor was her second husband and a great scholar, and she aspired to have him become rosh yeshiva. I called for Yitzhak of Melnik because of his great influence against Rav Yaakov, and because he was a powerful backer of Rav Avigdor. I was also sent to the opposite camp, that of Rav Yaakov, as a spy, to see who came to study with him. I was told to even listen to his lecture, and I remember that he spoke of "asmakhtah." Before the decision, a quarrel broke out between the boy Mordoshkovitz and Yitzhak of Melnik. The former complained about the latter that he wanted Rav Avigdor, but in fact he hadn't made up his mind. **[This is all as my father recorded it; the specifics may have been lost to the mists of time—Ed.]** In the end the decision was reached to officially oppose Rav Yaakov.

After this event, I received a notice from my parents telling me that because of the second expulsion, they had left Brisk and had traveled to Minsk with the great Rav Haim Brisker.

My father told me that when my grandfather was at the station with Rav Haim, the two of them walked up and down the platform while waiting for the train to pull in. Of course they were discussing Torah. My grandfather stopped walking, and, facing Rav Haim, told him: "I want you to know that from now on I will be wearing *tefillin* on chol ha-mo'ed Succos (the intermediate days of a 9-day holiday), unlike what I have been doing until now, which was out of respect for your minhag." Upon being asked why he planned to change his custom, my grandfather replied that he had based the decision on his personal experience of walking through the city and watching what people did. More people, he found, went out to work and behaved in a non-holiday fashion than treated that period of time as a holiday. If they treated the days like weekdays, then they needed to wear tefillin as if they were weekdays. My father continued to follow this decision until he moved back to Israel in 1975 after his earlier sojourn there. When he was berated in shul for doing this, he decided to put on his tefillin at home, and then go to shul to pray without them.

Because of this and the depressing situation of the yeshiva, I left Volozhin, heading for Minsk. Before I left, my grandfather, the Gaon Rav Avraham, died. His death depressed the entire city. I remember that there were eight eulogies that day and among those speaking were yeshiva students. His death affected me too, and it seems that I was inspired to be more pious.

In Volozhin my father found a rebbe for me, a Bialystocker. He was very handsome, and my sister Feigl was very interested, but it didn't work out. Many years ago I found out that he had moved to Boro Park. I met him there, but he did not understand what I was saying in Yiddish, not even when I said it in Hebrew. He was involved only with money. I was very disappointed. Then I had Rav Yokhn. I later met him in Bialystok—a diamond of a man.

Q. How long did you study with Rav Yokhn?

A. Until we had to return—a couple of years—until the war was over. We were not treated well by Feigl at my grandparents' house. She even spoke against Father— "You came here [only] to eat...." It was awful! And later she was able to marry because of Father's *yichus*.

Q. So this was the Rudensky family—Feigl Rudensky was Sorke's niece?

A. Yes.

The Bobruisk Chapter

From Volozhin I traveled to Minsk, the capital city of White Russia, on the heels of the news that I had received that my parents were there after being expelled from Brisk. The "MeOr HaGola," ha-Rav Haim Soloveitchik, was settled in Minsk. After hearing that there was an outstanding young Torah scholar in the city of Bobruisk in Minsk province, my parents traveled there with me with the idea of putting me under his wing for the study of Torah.. I was accepted by the young man, Rav Shlomo the Pritzi from Poritz, whose excellent reputation was agreed upon by all. Now, at the age of twelve, I studied with him one to two hours a day, but not with the enthusiasm hoped for by my parents.

Each Erev Pesach I traveled with my father to Minsk at the request of Rav Haim to participate in the baking of matzot, an activity that took on a different form with him, with all of the dignity and beauty of a lovely play. My father also wished to bake his own matzot there, which was impossible to do as meticulously in Bobruisk—it needed the sharp supervision of a rabbi with experience, for sometimes a tiny bit of chametz can fall into the dough despite all the care that can be taken.

My grandfather refused to wear modern western suits or hats, but he also did not wear rabbinic garb. Rather, he chose to wear the long black *kapote* that was long-established traditional garb for the men of Eastern Europe. Of course, at one time that actually had been a modern look, but after hundreds of years it had become "traditional." Every photograph of him that we have shows him in this black coat, and wearing a brimmed cap or, once in a while, a Russian-style Cossack fur hat. He also had a winter coat lined with fur on the inside, with only the fur of the collar showing; it would have been immodest to let more of the fur be visible.

My grandfather never posed for pictures. Whatever photographs exist of him were taken at times when he was oblivious to the photographer, generally thinking over a question that was asked of him. Or, in the case of a famous image of him with Rav Haim Soloveichik's son Reb Velvel, he was too polite to move out of the way. The only pictures that he posed for were the ones taken when my father visited Brest-Litovsk in 1937, the year after his marriage, and a year before my grandmother died.

There was also another reason for these trips that was no less important: when I was in Minsk, I had to undergo meticulous testing by Rav Haim on Talmud. I usually excelled. I remember that one time my father complained to him that my envy of my relatives who knew Hebrew well was distracting me from my Talmud studies. The Rav advised my father to teach me to read the Torah, and to have me chant it in public, so that I coulds gain the respect I so desired. And so it was! When I returned home, my father began to teach me proper Torah trope, and it wasn't long before I stood on the big synagogue's "bima" and sang clearly and beautifully in my sweet boy's voice, especially the "haftarot." My yearning was fulfilled, for reading the Torah brought me the respect I wanted.

There was one important event that greatly influenced my later development that I clearly remember from that period. When I was in Minsk, one erev Pesach [early in the day], I went out of the rabbi's house and saw that from the nearby jail prisoners were emerging, making a great noise. It was noon. I was only a boy and did not understand what was going on. I watched and saw that the men leaving the prison looked strange, with pale and skinny faces. Some were barefoot, and some had nothing on but a shirt or pants. It was a strange sight which I did not comprehend. Looking back on it now, I realize that these men had been imprisoned for days or years, eating only hard bread and drinking water, and when they were freed, like a dog off his leash, they did not know where to go. Among the freed prisoners I saw the mashgiach of Yeshivat Volozhin, Rav Avraham Drushkovits, who had been imprisoned because he had forged identity cards. This had caused an uproar, because to do such a thing caused a "hilul ha-shem" (desecration of God) and was damaging to the holy status of the administrators and mashgichim of the yeshivas.

The agitation leading to the Russian Revolution made a big impression on me while I was in Minsk. Revolution?, I wondered. What was this, and for what? I knew nothing of it, but I inquired into it. What did these things mean to me, a lad? There were many demonstrations in the city, and red flags led each march. There were songs and slogans, rows of men and women arm in arm striding on the streets, and noise ... it was a true upheaval. It was all very exciting for a young person, and filled me with joy and satisfaction.

In Bobruisk I began to be interested in social issues, but I had no background to help me learn about them. I remember that there were two warring factions in the city: one was named the Zionists, and the other was the Bundists. **[The Bund—the General Jewish Workers Union—was founded in 1897, the same year as the World Zionist Organization—Ed.]** *At the head of each faction stood two brothers-in-law: Niakhka Yokhbid led the Bundists and Levin the photographer led the Zionists. Both were big men and excellent orators. The first was all veins and skin and nothing more, but he worked for his cause to his last strength, even though after each speech they attacked him. I was said that when he was imprisoned in 1905 as a revolutionary, they cut off his [indecipherable]. The two orators fought with sharpness and vigor. I used to come and go among the Zionists, but was more often with the Bundists because I felt closer to them. I remember that once I participated with the Zionists in a theatrical presentation of "The Eternal*

Song" at the invitation of Levin, portraying the grandson. I did this without my parents' knowledge.

My studies with the student Shlomo the Pritzi continued with stubbornness and difficulty, because I didn't have any special desire for it.... Yet despite this, in one year I completed Masekhet Bava Metzia, and with the completion of the Masekhet a celebration took place at my home. They prepared for me a special party and invited the father-in-law of Rav Moshe Mordekhai, Rav Yechezkel from Novoridok, who was then in Bobruisk, to attend. I gave what I was told was a "superb speech," and this satisfied my dear parents, relatives, and myself. I wanted then to immerse myself in the Hebrew classes of the Zionists—not so much from a desire to know Hebrew as due to envy of the sons of our relatives who were studying Russian in the Gymnasia and knew Hebrew well. However, my parents opposed this plan, and in order to fulfill my desire they hired a teacher—Reb Zalman the "Magid" of Brisk—to teach me Prophets. The man had a reputation for his knowledge of Bible, but he could not teach in Hebrew, as I required. My desire to know Hebrew came from my envy of my cousins the Barishanskys. Their family home was one of Enlightenment in the true sense of the new concept. The sons, who were my age, attended the gymnasium, but also knew Hebrew and Hebrew literature. They knew all the latest ideas. Under the influence of Tolstoy's books they became aware of the sins of "cruelty to living creatures." I used to discuss *this topic with them and was influenced by them. I began to behave like them, but I could not last, as my lifestyle was not like theirs—they were wealthy and had many fruits and dairy dishes, but I suffered from hunger. So, after four days, I regretted adopting the idea of vegetarianism and decided to eat meat and fish like everyone else.*

I remember that at around that time one of them became Bar-Mitzva, and at the feast prepared in his honor he gave a beautiful speech in Hebrew. I stood, looked at his face, and envied him greatly. I loved their house and visited it often. I had a special relationship with their young daughter Sima, a student who was only in the second year of the Russian gymnasium yet already knew a great deal of Hebrew. The girl was very pretty, and she showed me special affection. I kissed her many times and she kissed me, but in private.... I remember that once I kissed her quickly on Yom Kippur. She felt guilty about that, because of the holiness of the day.

Meanwhile I too reached the age of thirteen on 25 Heshvan 1916. My parents, following tradition, made a lavish party for me. They invited everyone important in the yeshiva world and in the city, as well as town leaders and all the yeshiva students from the Bet Midrash of Rav Margalin. I prepared well before the party, for it was obligatory to speak before the large crowd. For my speech, my father taught me a difficult sugya in connection with tefillin ("tzitz u-metzakh") from Shaagat Arye and of course, also from the Beit Ha-Levi, as well as some sharp items that I had learned from my rebbe, the student Shlomo the Pritzi Poritz. **[This refers to a piece of responsa literature regarding forgetting that one is wearing tefillin, the 38th teshuva of the Sha'agat Arye—Ed.]** *I was excellent. In the middle of my speech, I was interrupted and challenged. They threw questions at me and I responded quickly and intelligently. This party remains in my memory forever, in part because of the gifts given to me. One gift given by my cousin the Dayan Rav Yosef was a Tanakh, which I still have and which I guard as a treasure.*

Q. We are up to the time of your Bar-Mitzva.

A. The Bar-Mitzva was in Bobruisk. I studied all of *Bava Metzia* with R Shlomo Heiman—he was the only one I studied with in Bobruisk. I said a little Torah of his, and then I spoke of tzitz u-metzakh from the *Shaagat Arye*. It was very complicated and Father had told me that he had spoken on this topic at his Bar-Mitzva, so I wanted to also, as his son. It was very complicated. And then I gave a little of Father's Torah. Not mine.

My father told me that my grandfather memorized the entire Talmud. He memorized it to such a degree that he could cross-reference anything that came up in terms of *halakhic* questions. Not one of his descendants has inherited this capability, although many did inherit aspects of his analytical abilities.

In order to deal with issues that were of the modern period, especially connected with new technologies, my grandfather had to master an understanding of these new technological advances. One of his most famous responsa dealt with the question of whether or not it was permissible to use a refrigerator on Shabbat.* He had to understand not only the workings of electricity, but also the principles behind what causes the machine to automatically turn itself on via the thermostat. He interviewed engineers and asked them pertinent questions. Then he applied the principles of talmudic law to what he had learned and ruled that refrigerators could indeed be used on Shabbat, thereby laying the groundwork for all later *halakhic* decisions connected with thermostats, electricity, and modern technology in general.

After the Bar-Mitzva, Rav Isser Zalman Meltzer was passing through Bobruisk. This was a scholar who had learned with Father in Volozhin. He embraced Father and kissed him. Father did not kiss back: he kissed no one. He saw me and grabbed me to test me. When he saw that I knew all of Bava Metzia, he said, "It is not right for him to be here. Yes, you have Rav Shlomo Heiman, but he needs the spirit of a yeshiva. He is all alone here. It is as though he is on an island. I will take him to Slutzk." [**R. Isser Zalman Meltzer headed a branch of Slobodka Yeshiva that opened in Slutzk in**

---

* See *HaPardes* 8:3 (June 1934).

1897. **Slobodka stressed musar, or reform of social values, as a way of meeting the challenges of modernity—Ed.]**

"On one condition," my father said. "You will hire for him a gemara teacher, because I want him to have a good basis for studying alone."

So I went to Slutzk, and the Slutzker Rav Isser Zalman, with Rav Aharon Kotler, his son-in-law, hired a teacher for me: Rav Shach (who is now famous in Ponevezh), who was then known as "the Vabulniker." We stayed together in an inn and he learned with me, and after a short time he went to Rav Aharon and Rav Isser Zalman and told them, "I don't want to take any money—he doesn't need a teacher!" So Rav Aharon said: "So, he doesn't need any help and can learn alone?" And he took out a gemara, Bava Kama 76, where there are two lines of gemara and a huge Tosfot, and he told me to prepare it alone. I did it in a few hours, and I knew it, and he said, "You do not need a teacher!" At eleven years old! **[He was in fact thirteen—Ed.]** *Alone!* **[The Lithuanian Yeshiva system was geared toward independent study—Ed.]**

A few weeks after the Bar-Mitzva there was an assembly of rabbis in the city. Among them was Rav Isser Zalman, the rabbi of Slutzk. Upon hearing of my talmudic knowledge, he requested of my father to send me to his yeshiva. His argument was that if I remained where I was, I would be exposed to bad culture—I needed the structure of a yeshiva. My father agreed, and I traveled with Rav Isser Zalman to Slutzk.

The outbreak of the revolution in Minsk and the escape of the prisoners took place after my Bar-Mitzva and the speech that I gave at the festive meal. The difficult sugya that I learned from the talented yeshiva student Rav Shlomo Hapritzi I debated with the "light of the diaspora," Rav Haim Soloveitchik, who deconstructed my entire Torah construct, but ended up very satisfied with my interpretation and pleased that I had debated with him so passionately. This was the last occasion on which I spent time in his company, for that year the Bolshevik Revolution occurred. **[He may have confused the Bolshevik Revolution with the March Revolution of 1917, four months after his Bar-Mitzvah—Ed.]** *The Germans had conquered that area and it was impossible to travel there, and my dear father did not travel that year to bake matza. After Pesach, we received a telegram from Rav Haim that he wanted to see Father before he left for Otwock —it seems that his heart informed him that this parting would be their last—so, after much effort, my father got permission to travel to Minsk for a single day for this farewell. He (R. Haim) was quite weak in those days, and he shared the bitterness of his situation with my dear father, who was his true friend from the day he left Volozhin Yeshiva. As he said, "his soul was bound up with his soul" all of his life.*

It is hard to describe this parting in words. It was one of true friends who each possessed a clear understanding that this was final and that they would never see each other again. And so it was. Within a year, the news spread that Rav Haim had died in Otwock. In the newspapers it was reported that a few hours before his death, he had requested that a telegram be sent to my beloved father, with a request that he pray for him, but to our chagrin there was no opportunity to send it before he died.

Q. When you moved back to Brisk, you moved back into the same house?

A. Yes. We were refugees in Bobruisk. Rav Shapiro's son ran up to Father in the street and blurted out that Rav Haim had died. Father almost fainted. He had no sense—he should have at least waited to tell him in the house, and spoken carefully.

A month later the Poles took Bobruisk and Brisk. Ten men came as a delegation from the community and brought a tzav *rabbanus* to Father telling him that he should be the Rav of Brisk. Mother was so happy. But Father said that Rav Haim had given him a hint that R Velvel, Rav Haim's younger son, should be the Rav, so he could not accept it. But the community did not want R Velvel because it was hard to deal with him. He was a big makhmir (follower of stringencies in Jewish law).

Q. But the situation remained the same, only now it was Rav Velvel who lived downstairs?

A. It was the same, but we suffered from his wife, Alte— *tzarot*, because she was not a nice woman. She was killed, in Vilna, by the Nazis. Her four sons are in Jerusalem.

The Slutzk Chapter

I came to Slutzk escorted by Rav Isser Zalman at the beginning of winter [1916/1917]. I lived, at first, in his house, but when he realized that I had to be supervised because of my (to him) unpleasant tendencies, he gave me to the care of the students Babulnik and Hasiniyatzo'i.

Rabbi Isser Zalman Meltzer (1870-1953) studied in Volozhin under Rav Hayyim Soloveitchik and the Netziv, and later under the Hafetz Haim. In 1897, Rav Natan Zvi Finkel, the rosh yeshiva of Slobodka Yeshiva, appointed him head of an advanced branch yeshiva in Slutzk.

Slobodka Yeshiva was founded in ca.1881 by Rav Natan Zvi Finkel, and grew rapidly upon absorbing many former students of the Volozhin Yeshiva after it was closed by the Russian government. Rav Finkel molded the yeshiva's unique focus on musar (ethics) texts, and delivered weekly musar lectures to all of the students. He created a new form of *mashgiach*, supervisor, and the man who held it served as an ethics teacher, emphasizing self-discipline. This emphasis on *musar* caused a split in the yeshiva in 1897, and the followers of Rav Finkel and his appointee Rav

Moshe Mordechai Epstein renamed their school Yeshiva Knesset Yisrael, after the founder of the *musar* movement, Rav Yisrael Lipkin (Salanter). The others called their new yeshiva Knesset Bet Yitzhak, after Rav Yitzhak Elchahan Spektor of Kovna. As the years passed, Rav Finkel appointed more heads of the yeshiva, including his son Rav Moshe Finkel and his son-in-law Rav Yitzhak Sher. When World War I brought the battlefield to Slobodka, the yeshiva moved first to Minsk and then to Kremenchug in the Ukraine, where it remained until 1921, when it returned to Slobodka.

He tended more towards the approach of Rav Yozl of the Navorodok Yeshiva, and the former followed Rav Notte Hirsh of Slobodka's yeshiva Knesset Israel. I was housed in a private home that the rabbi rented for the three of us. He also hired the student Zelig of Strovin, a great scholar and excellent teacher, to instruct me. On Shabbat I ate with the Rav De-Mata (Isser Zalman) and that day was when I was tested on all I had learned the preceding week. The examiners included not only the Rav but also his son-in-law the rosh yeshiva, the "Ilui" R Aharon of Svislovitzch. In this way, half the winter passed.

In Russia, the elections for Parliament began. Electioneering was in full swing among the movements and parties, especially among the Zionists, who aimed to win a recognized place in Parliament. The traditional Jews went

*to the elections separately. The dispute between them grew.
Even the yeshiva did not remain passive in the midst of all
of this. Headed by the rosh yeshiva, the students actively
participated in the arguments in which the entire Jewish and
non-Jewish community was immersed, in preparation for the
elections.*

*I too did not stay out of this "holy work," and of course
I worked against the Zionists. This anti-Zionist attitude came
from my education at home and from Rav Haim Soloveitchik,
who also felt this way. The traditional parties did not fear the
external enemy—the leftist parties—because, they felt, their
influence was distant and not fundamental. But they greatly
feared the Zionists, the internal enemy, who undermined the
basis of religion. They were more dangerous because they
knew how to attack and destroy. Out of this fear grew enmity
toward the Zionists, and this influenced me, and I opposed
them as well. Another cause of my opposition was the anti-
Zionist arguments presented by the leftist parties, which
I also continued to follow. With these weapons, I went to the
battlefield to begin to fight for the Orthodox. My work was
fruitful and important, for the site of my battle was next to the
ballot box, the place where the fateful votes were cast. My job
in this place was difficult, for there all the various lies about
our preferred candidates were spread more effectively than at
dozens of the best speeches. I fulfilled my task successfully,
and thanks in part to my work the Orthodox won a big victory.*

This work made me famous in the city and outside it, made me very popular, and brought respect to me.

I remember standing once in the courtyard of the nagid (the richest man) of the city, where there was a voting station, and I was defending the Orthodox party, when the son of the nagid, Yoshke, who had also participated in the debate but on the side of the Zionists, came out and began to debate with me. I, of course, with the wealth of my arguments, won, and for this he invited me into his house. He honored me with a cup of tea. His parents took an interest in me, and asked if I was studying Haskalah. I explained to them that I had not had the opportunity nor the means for that subject. As a result of that conversation, I remember, on one Shabbat the gvir (rich man) came to the house of the Rav Damata (Isser Zalman), and when he saw me sitting at the table, he suggested that the rabbi hire a teacher of Russian for me. The rabbi, of course, opposed this, using a combative tone to the gvir, and that ended that. The fact that the Rav answered in this way to the gvir had the opposite effect on me than might be anticipated: instead of worrying about and mourning the fact that each attempt of mine failed, I threw myself into the sea of the Talmud, so sweet and deep, and accomplished a great deal at that time.

I got to know one of the greatest men involved in the revival of the yeshiva. He was named Tzvi, and he was the son of a man named Rav Isser Zalman, a "ba'al teshuva" (repenter) under the influence of the Navorodoks and a lover of musar.

The *musar* movement arose in the nineteenth century within the context of Lithuanian Jewish culture. It stressed both strict ethical behavior and *halakha*. Inspired by Rav Yisrael Lipkin (also called Yisrael Salanter), it was originally directed at the upper circle of the community, and was meant to help them meet the challenges presented by the Haskalah movement and Hasidism. Another important issue it addressed was how to sustain a rigorous traditional life based on *halakha* and intellectuality in a milieu of increasing poverty. When their philosophy failed to attract the older members of the community, the *musar* movement's leaders began to focus on the education of the young, especially in the yeshivot. However, this new maneuvering led to sharp opposition from traditional yeshiva leadership, represented in part by Rav Yitzhak Elchanan Spektor of Kovno, who was opposed to the *musar* movement in its institutional forms. Still, the *musar* movement prevailed, and it is this form of learning that is more popular in the modern day.

The movement's educational methodology included reciting passages from ethical books, biblical verses, and sayings aloud, to a melody, in a manner which would evoke emotions. At least half an hour a day was devoted to reading the texts, in unison, at twilight, using the same plaintive melody. The *mashgiach* held a weekly lecture for all of the students on a moral topic.

The movement was successful in counteracting secularizing trends, but, as with all movements, there emerged both a maximalist group and a minimalist one. The minimalist group, made up of what were called the "Slobodka-style" yeshivot, in which students would spend less time involved in such emotional exercises, created a collective sense of identity. The maximalist group was called the "Novardok-style" yeshivot. Its leader, Rav Yosef Yozl Horowitz, not only increased the hours devoted to studying *musar* texts, but required students to learn self-discipline by performing tasks meant to control vanity and materialism.

I had never met such remarkable people. Their method of learning musar, the "Bursa'ot," influenced me: these were discussions on the topic of "fear of God," held while strolling in front of the yeshiva or in the market. I was intrigued by the sad voices of lonely students with their eyes lifted to the sky, the various melodies used while studying musar *statements like "Better to be a fool all one's days than to be evil before God even for an hour." The students brought pain and great fear, and the echo of their voices pierced deeply into a heart and soul that at the time was like a smooth blackboard, impressed by each whisper. The long prayers [said alone] in their sad and heart-wrenching voices, the strange movements—both had a great influence on me and prepared the ground for what happened to me in the future....*

Before Pesach I received a command from my parents to come home for the holiday and to bring with me flour for shmura matza. I bought it and sat on the hired wagon, along with a number of other men. Among them was the brother of the rav of Bobruisk, the student Asher Shapira, who was in Slutzk for the sole purpose of buying flour for matza, and purchased a great deal of it. The trip was not a peaceful one. By that time the Poles had conquered Bobruisk, where my parents were residing, and the entire area was in a state of siege and battle. The wagon was endangered as it entered the large wild forest just as night fell. We saw cavalry in the distance and did not know whose it was, but as they came a little closer there was a shout and shooting. We did not know who was attacking. We were terrified and leaped off the wagon, throwing ourselves completely on the ground like dead people without a word. The soldiers, as they came up to us, beat us with their whips, looted everything, and left. They took my bag with my clothing and belongings, and the matza flour as well. Sighing from pain and shaking from fear, we traveled on until, breathless, we came to the city. There, the news of the attack on us quickly spread, and the city of Bobruisk was upside-down [the Hebrew word here is *navokha,* a reference to the city of-Shushan at the time of Esther and Mordechai—Ed.].

As a result of this unfortunate event and due to the looting, which had left me without a change of clothing, I could not return immediately after Pesach to the yeshiva in Slutzk. While I tarried in Bobruisk, I had constant internal battles. The primary reason for these battles was the lovely girl Sima Brishansky; my relationship with her was now influenced by my winter of musar in Slutsk. In my mind I had developed the idea that envy, lust, and honor remove a man from this world—and I was battling all three of those feelings. But my evil inclination overcame me, and my relationship with Sima remained as before.

After Shavuot, I returned to Slutzk and was housed in the apartment in which I had lived during the previous winter. On Shabbat, once again, I ate at the table of Rav Isser Zalman. The yeshiva, which during the winter had been located in a different place—because the Russian army had taken over the building during the war—was now back in its home, below the city amidst the fields and grass. The yeshiva had been purposely placed here when it had been founded to remove the students from the noisy city life—not only to protect them from the sounds of people coming and going, but also so that their hearts would not be attracted to paths other than those of the rules of musar.

Because the student Zelig of Strubin who had taught me during the winter had just married, I studied with a student from Bubolnik who lived with me. The glorious summer season, which was calling to us to leave the walls of the yeshiva and come closer to nature, caused the "seder" (curriculum) in the yeshiva to progress slowly. It ended very late, and the students were tired from the long day and the heat of the place, so they often left to walk a bit around the yeshiva in the grassy fields, to breathe some clear air, to invigorate their hearts and lungs, and to enjoy the beauty of nature. I too strolled, but my enjoyment did not last long. The spirit of musar began to fill the yeshiva, and it overtook almost everything in its path.

The instigator of this change was the student Yaakov of Slutzk. He was the good-looking son of a poor harness-maker. Years before he had been taken into the army and sent to the battlefield. There he had been badly wounded in both his legs. He became a cripple, leaning on two canes, and returned from the army to become a "Nawardok" and a fiery baal musar. In the late afternoons, before evening fell, when everyone was bone-tired and closed their gemaras to walk to the fields, embracing nature and feeling like tiny parts of the gorgeous cosmos, during a season when summer knocked at the window, calling us to leave the walls of the city and its choking dust for grass, to dance on it and all the flowering vegetation—that was when this student, leaning on his two crutches, would convince the young boys to stay in the yeshiva to listen to his musar, which was deep and penetrated the heart and the soul. His powerful arguments changed your view on all this beauty. You ceased looking at the environment that you had appreciated, and viewed it as a net and trap aimed at snaring you. We sat around the tables, and Yaakov would stand, leaning on his crutches. With a loud but melancholy voice he pierced the soul and explained to us "the miseries—hevel havalim" **(this is a referrence to the Book of Kohelet—Ed.)** of this world and the search for enjoyment. After that, you *would not look at the green fields but at heaven, or into the Vale of Tears.... His strength influenced all of us, and I too became a* baal musar.

Meanwhile, the month of Elul approached. In that month, issues of the Day of Judgment darkened the yeshiva. The walls of the yeshiva and the people within them took on a new form, that of pain and suffering and weeping. In every corner you could feel that it was the season of repentance, and that all were breathing with the difficulty borne of internal danger, fear for the soul, and knowledge that the future was covered in fog. In those days, Rav Isser Zalman himself dedicated himself to rousing repentance. He was an expert in this work. Morning and night he would speak of the approaching Day of Judgment, and the preparations for it that had to be done in our hearts. With himself as an example, he roused us. One example he gave rings in my ears even today—that of a poor lamb ready for slaughter, who bleats loudly and feels that it is her last moment—"Who knows who this lamb is, who is going to die?," he would ask us. He would look at us and for an answer there would come only sobbing. Our tears wet the floor of the house. He would repeat and stress the greatest sin of all: [laziness, for] the Jew must get used to the strictness of law and not to its ease, for worship of God is difficult and it is with great suffering that man must fulfill God's will. He also gave a dire warning against one more thing: plagiarizing a colleague's work and passing it off as one's own. These things greatly touched the young people, for they always aimed for great ideas. His words were extremely influential: they entered the very soul.

I did not go home for Rosh Hashana, for it would have been simply despicable to leave during for days that were so important at the yeshiva, the nest of prayers and repentance. I remained in Slutsk through Yom Kippur. We celebrated the holiday within the walls of the yeshiva, studying musar *and saying fearful and awesomely agonizing prayers. I remember that on the first night of Rosh Hashana, as evening came, we did not pray maariv immediately as we usually did, but instead had a general class on* musar *and awakening. After that we prayed a maariv that was replete with weeping and general crying. So passed the ten days of teshuva in Slutzk.* **[The days between and including Rosh Hashana and Yom Kippur are referred to as the "Ten Days of Teshuva" or the "Ten Days of Repentance—Ed.]**

I went to Bobruisk, to be with my parents, for Succot. After Succot I could not return immediately to Slutzk because of my participation in a great occasion—the wedding of my sister Feigl on 5 Heshvan 1917. The groom was the ilui from the Volozhin yeshiva, Rav Moshe Reuven, of whom I wrote above in a passage regarding his dispute with Rav Yaakov in that yeshiva. This match took place after the agreement of Rav Haim and after some tests my father gave the groom during a visit to Volozhin. After these tests, my father attested that Rav Moshe Reuven was worthy and suitable to marry my sister. The wedding, of course, was replete with the special entertainment of a "learned wedding." The most important men from the world of learning and yeshivot were invited and participated, and it was an outstanding event. This was during the time that the Germans, who had ousted the Bolsheviks, ruled that area.

All of the Reguer sisters were pretty, but although they resembled each other in appearance, they had very different personalities and ambitions. The eldest sister, Feigl, had the responsibilities of helping her mother put on her at an early age. She was literate in Yiddish, as all the girls were, but helping in the house was an enormous burden on her, and while her younger sisters could aspire to become more educated and work as nurses, she set her mind on escaping her circumstances through marriage. As the eldest daughter, she was also pressured to marry early, so as not to mar the chances of her younger sisters, who were not far behind her in age.

There were many young yeshiva students who were more than willing to marry the daughter of Rav Simcha Zelig. Feigl was introduced to a well-screened few, and met them one at a time in the traditional Jewish manner: by taking a quick look at them across a roomful of people. She chose the best-looking one. Even from the pictures you can tell that he was handsome. Sadly, as she later discovered, looks don't mean everything. The wedding took place in due time, and the young couple, with no money of their own, moved "temporarily" into the second bedroom, with Feigl's younger sisters, including the youngest, who was a good fifteen years younger than the others, moved out to sleep in the tiny room. Everyone tolerated this arrangement because it was supposed to be temporary, as Moshe Reuven Gulewski was supposed to get his *smicha* and find a place for himself and his family. My father's sleeping area, when he was home, was under the staircase. However, Moshe Reuven and Feigl never ended up moving out of the house.

Immediately after the seven days of celebration following the wedding, I returned to Slutzk. Rav Isser Zalman began to check on the spiritual state of the yeshiva students. He inspected us and found that the spirituality of the yeshiva was very low, and so he demanded a new strengthening from those of us who could withstand it.

Until Chanuka, the person in charge of musar was the limping leaner on crutches—the student Yaakov of Slutzk, who I described above. For Chanuka each year, the yeshiva traditionally became a theater, and the yeshiva boys spent these days with joy. All the people of the town—women and children too—came to the yeshiva to watch the wonderful plays put on by the students, to listen to timely speeches, songs, and jokes. In the middle of the holiday this year, there was a rumor in the yeshiva that the Rav had sent a telegram to Rav Yozl, who was then in the city of Homel, asking him to come imbue the yeshiva's students with the spirit of musar and strengthen them in the worship of God. This rumor turned out to be true, and on one of the days of Chanuka, Rav Yozl came to Slutzk with his strong-armed men, young men with strong oratory abilities—and strong fists. I had already heard of Rav Yozl, but I did not know of his methods. My father also had spoken of him, saying that the Ha-Tzfira newspaper wrote about him and called him "he of the breaches," because the house in which he had lived alone in the woods for twelve years had two holes through which food was placed: one for meat and one for dairy.

Rav Yozl's arrival in Slutzk greatly influenced everyone, even his opponents, who respected not his musar method but the man, the great thinker. Right after he arrived he began his work—teaching the method of musar, with immediate results. The atmosphere changed—not only did he teach musar to all of us in formal classes, he would invite students to debate his method of study and life. His basic belief was that one must reject this world and expose its rottenness. This world, he would say, is just a prozdor (corridor) to the next, and so it is one's obligation to recognize one's goals here in the prozdor: preparation via mitzvot and good deeds, which are the only deciding things for men. Particularly important are personal deeds, which will act as constant weapons in the human in his war against his evil inclination, which is constantly fighting *for his soul. This clear recognition, to which man must pay attention, required constant and stubborn actions against the evil inclination, which is there to ensnare him. Thus man must educate himself and strengthen himself by various tests to be able to battle "envy, lust, and honor, which are lures to sin." One accomplishes this not by running away, but by meeting and conquering these enemies. Positive attributes of man are: submission, distancing from honor, and modesty, and a person's true task in this world of hevel havalim is to keep God's commandments in their entirety, to live a life of* musar, *holiness, and separation from this world's enjoyments, and to elevate the soul to the highest steps possible.*

What emerges from this set of ideas is the concept that keeping what is written in the Torah and Talmud is important, but even more so is keeping what is in the books of musar, *such as* Hovat ha-Levavot *and* Mesilat Yesharim. *Knowledge of Torah—even on the level of a gaon—was not in his eyes particularly estimable and was not a measuring stick of Judaism; he labeled it bitul ha-gaoniyut. There is a special value placed on the life of asceticism —distance from the evils of life, which enables purity of thought, which brings man close to God. Many opposed the means of realizing this approach, for the details of bringing this battle with the evil inclination to fruition for the yeshiva as a whole were decided by a committee which gave each student a specific task. Some examples were: to enter a bathhouse and ask the price of* a liter of tzitzit, to beg for money, to roll a large barrel in the middle of the most beautiful and busy streets of the town, to buy 1/4 of a liter of oil for the Chanuka lamp, to walk in the street with ragged clothing and tzitzit hanging out of the shirt, to turn one's coat inside out, and to do other such insane things, as they did in the large and beautiful cities of Russia. The students asked Rav Yozl about the nature of these tasks and about the "chilul hashem be rabim" that they engendered, for Torah scholars embarrassed both themselves and the respect for the Torah, as is written by the scholars: "A Torah scholar with a stain on his clothing deserves death." Rav Yozl would reply, "A stain on the heart is a thousand times worse than a stain on a coat!" He felt that if a man was not be tested once in his life, he would never be able to battle the evil inclination, and that engaging in these tests was the only way to a life of rectitude, musar, and righteousness.

Rav Yozl lived in the house of Rav Isser Zalman, and since I was one of Rav Isser Zalman's extended family, he knew my name, and that I was the son of one of the leading Torah scholars of the world. He started conversations with me and tried to influence me to follow his ways, for it would have been a great victory if they could "convert" the son of a rabbi of my father's status to be one of them. I heard that despite their preaching and qualities, some of them came to a village to recruit and when they did not have an easy time of it, they forcibly grabbed the boys by the arms and stuck them in their wagon and took them away. Obviously they never returned but became Nawardokayim.

Until mid-winter, I studied with the student Babulnikai, but one day the son-in-law of Rav Isser Zalman, Rav Aharon Pines, the Ilui of Sabislovitz, called me and on his own assigned me a "kri'a"—a group of pages of gemara with all the commentaries, which I was to read and then be tested on. I remember that the "sugya" was in Baba Kama, p. 10. He set a deadline, at which point I came to be tested. I knew the entire sugya backward and forward, and on my test I performed so well in both depth and breadth that Rav Aharon Pines ordered that I should study alone. This announcement made a strong impression on the yeshiva, especially on the other younger students, because it was a tradition that even the best students were never told at such a young age—fifteen—to study alone without help or supervision. I informed my dear father of this instruction, and he was very satisfied, and agreed to allow it. However, fearing that I would learn less, he ordered me to study some more with the older students in addition to working independently.

In the middle of the winter the Germans left the area and the Bolsheviks moved in. Before Pesach the Bolshevik newspaper Der Weker announced the sudden death of Rav Haim Soloveitchik in Otwock. When I returned home I couldn't stop crying, and I eulogized this giant on whose knees, so to speak, I was educated, and who served as a guide and leader during my boyhood.

The influence of Rav Yozl in the field of musar, and my elevation in the level of my studies, awoke in me the desire to travel to Yeshivat Knesset Israel of Slobodka, which at that time was in Kremenchug in the Ukraine, and which was known as one of the greatest yeshivas in the world.

Before Pesach I traveled home to Bobruisk. While there, I told my dear father of my decision, and with his agreement—though my mother was against it because of the distance and because of the abnormal times we were living in—I left Bobruisk right after the holiday and set out for Kremenchug. I was later told that my mother cried all night over her wandering son, as though her heart told her that my fate would be bitter indeed.

Q. Why did you pick Slobodka?

A. Because, even though Father did not think highly of *baalei musar*—and it took me years to understand that he was right—I was deeply affected by the *baalei musar*.

Q. You went on the train by yourself?

A. Mother cried all night. Grandmother was in Kremenchug. Zeitchik had a brother there. He had died, and I took over his room. Afterwards I had great suffering from this, because I read one of his books and I did not want to affect anyone's memories of it by admitting it was his.

Q. Who paid for the trip?

A. Father. Father always had money for learning. Esther and Golde were still single; Feigl was already married to

Moshe Reuven. I don't remember my brothers at home at all. Peshke was twenty months younger than me.

She (Mother) wrote to her mother that she had cried all night. She was very close to me and was very sensitive, a true mother.

Q. Was Kremenchug a big city?

A. Yes. I went through two pogroms there. It was in the midst of the Russian Revolution, and the civil war between the Whites and the Reds. I had the privilege of hearing Trotsky when he addressed the Cossacks for the first time, after saving us against the Whites (Denikintzim). I had never in my life heard such a speaker.

Q. How could you hear Trotsky speak? I thought you were a yeshiva *bochur*. You knew Russian?

A. Yes, I was a yeshiva *bochur*, but I was anxious to hear him. I understood what he said, with fire. And right after he finished speaking, all the Cossacks immediately went to the front and killed the Whites, who had made pogroms right and left in Kremenchug.

The Kremenchug Chapter

I came to Kremenchug in 1919, right after Pesach and I went to the house of my uncle, the Resh Metivta of Yeshiva Kremenchug, Rav Eliezer Yitzhak [Berman, who was married to Sorke's sister Dobke—Ed.]. *My teacher, too, lived there, Rav Shlomo the Pritzi [Heiman], who had married my cousin Feigl, daughter of Rav Yochanan of Volozhin. After his marriage, my teacher was appointed Rosh Metivta in place of my uncle Rav Eliezer Yitzhak (who had fled the wartime atmosphere). My grandmother, too, the pious Rotke, lived there. I was accepted to the Slobodka Yeshiva, Knesset Israel, only after many attempts, because it was the custom of the heads to make it difficult. They believed that if a student's entry only became possible after many attempts and hurdles, his attitude to the yeshiva would differ from if he had enjoyed an easy acceptance, and his learning would be more pleasing to the administrators.*

After a few weeks, the Grigorians conquered the city. Grigory was a Russian general who gathered around him many Russian soldiers. These were plain pillagers, searching for blood, loot, and murder. They fought the Bolsheviks. Their name was already infamous in that area, for it was known that wherever they trod, destruction and rivers of Jewish blood were left behind. When the news came to the city that the Grigorians were coming, the fear of death fell on all.

I remember that on the first night, when they arrived and darkness covered the earth, horrible screams arose from all sides of the city. The Grigorians were trying to steal everything, and those who refused to turn over their property were beaten half to death or even killed. The next morning, I—who did not yet know what a pogrom was—went to the yeshiva. All the yeshiva boys gathered there and we prayed, sobbing and wailing. We said various Psalms with great feeling, as though facing death—which in fact we were.

That same morning an event occurred in the city which terrified the Jews and caused specific anguish to me and my relatives. One of the students of "Knesset Yitzhak" yeshiva of Slobodka, which was near our yeshiva, was stopped in the street by a soldier, who asked him for his papers. When he saw the word "Talmudist," he thought that it meant "Communist." At that very moment, he told him to turn his head. There was one shot of his gun, and the student fell to the ground, rolling in his own blood. A Gentile woman who was standing there could not bear to stand by and watch as the boy died in great pain, and wanted to give him some water, but the murdering soldier wanted to kill her as well. After a few moments of agony the student's soul left for on-high.... He was the only son of the

Rav of Horotzel, and news of the murder spread like wildfire. When it reached my relatives, they almost died of fear that I was the one killed, because his coat was like mine.

Despite the danger of going out, the wife of my teacher Rav Shlomo the Pritzi, Feigl, went to the house of the rich man Schreier (Nagid), where I had gone from the yeshiva. When she saw me, her face lit up with joy and she cried, "Boruch ha-shem!! We all thought you were dead!" She told me of the rumor and the sad story, of which I had known nothing. A great fear gripped all of us over this murder, and we feared that the killers would attack us as well, for we could hear the screams of the rich people who were being attacked. I asked Schreier if, were I to be questioned, he would say I was his son, and asked my cousin to bring me any official document from the house. She was able to travel safely, for she looked like a Gentile woman. She went and brought me my identity card.

The attacks continued, coming as close as our courtyard, and I saw with my own eyes how a soldier grabbed a Jew and put his sword next to his neck—I thought that I would soon see a dead body, with its tongue licking the dust. I began to shake and convulse uncontrollably. [**Evidently, on this occasion the Jew was in the end not murdered—Ed.**]

Before evening, as the sun's last rays lapped the rich and lovely Ukraine, instead of the usual peace that came with sunset, fear and heavy trepidation filled my heart. The horrible pogroms *intensified, especially at night, in the moonshine. No one dared to go out. One innocent girl put her head out of the door and was de-capitated and her head rolled in the dust marked by a red trail....*

The screams rose and the Ukrainian night echoed with them. In the void of the atmosphere, a sharp sword filthy with Jewish blood floated, calling for vengeance on behalf of the pain of the children and their mothers. In the house where I was staying, we were all exhausted from five days' lack of sleep, and we fell on the floor in a daze. Suddenly a strong hand woke me and pulled me. I was so deeply asleep that I instinctively arose and cried, "They're here!! Death is hovering in the room!!" I ran out of the house in a panic.

This exit cost me dearly, for I was covered in sweat and the low temperature affected me severely. I caught a bad cold—fever gripped me, and I became terribly ill. The next day they brought me to the Christian hospital outside of town, where I was taken to the reception room until a doctor could come and examine me. I lay, as if in a faint, and felt nothing except when they put me on a stretcher. I only remember that the nurse came, stuck her nail into my finger, and blood began to flow. The drop of blood was examined, and it was found that I had shakhefet (typhus). I was put into the special typhus ward. I felt that my illness was growing strong, and that I myself was growing weak. Making matters even worse was the fact that I was all alone. I could not speak their language, and so could not request anything.

I remember that while we were still in the reception room, before my examination, there was a sudden noise— a bomb had landed in the hospital! Everyone began to cry and yell. That same day, a priest went to all the wards and held the cross in front of each sick person to be kissed. Even though I could not see clearly what the priest held, I instinctively felt NO: It is forbidden to kiss it. When he approached me and held out the cross, I pushed him aside with all of my strength. This was dangerous for me, for as I found out later, I could have been severely punished for such behavior. The act of pushing aside a cross during a time of pogroms! But in this case, the priest paid it no mind and left.

While in the hospital, I suffered from lack of food— they only served treif food and I couldn't and wouldn't eat it. They did not know the reason for my abstinence, and against my will they force-fed me treif milk.... Afterward, the yeshiva students came and brought me kosher food. They endangered themselves coming to the hospital, for any time a person left the city he could be killed. My aunt Dobke also came often to see me, along with Feigl, the wife of my teacher Rav Shlomo ha-Pritzi. When I saw them I was a bit comforted, and always asked them to pray for me. The only prayer I could think of was "Shir Ha-Maalot: mi ma'amakim kiratikha" ("From the depths I call out to You," Psalm 130), and we poured out our hearts in reciting it.

My understanding from the stories my father told me later in his life was that at first no one knew what had happened to my father, and there was chaos everywhere. There was great concern among our relatives, and my great-grandmother Rotke sent out one of her granddaughters, Feigl, who was angular, tall, and non-Jewish-looking, to look for him. With her head wrapped in a babushka to make her look like a Ukrainian woman, Feigl went to the local hospital and went from bed to bed, looking at the young men and boys who were there. She even made her way to the morgue. When she asked to see the patients in the last room in the hospital, the nurse said that these men were not the injured, but typhus patients. Feigl figured she would look at them as well, for what was one more ward, and entered the crowded room. And there was my father! He had been sent there, but the pogrom had broken out before word could be sent to his grandmother. Feigl rushed home, and his family provided my father with kosher food and company until the doctors dismissed him. He never forgot his debt to his cousin, and I remember her clearly, first from our visits to her on the Lower East Side when she was married to Rabbi Heiman, and then when I saw her in Tel Aviv, when she was married to Rabbi Unterman. It is interesting to note that her first marriage was arranged due to the *yichus* of being Simcha Zelig's niece. In fact she was not—she was Sorke's niece—but no one seemed to care. She had two wonderful husbands, despite not being a great beauty, which one might have expected would discourage matchmakers.

I remember on one occasion walking into her home in Tel Aviv, where I had been invited to spend Shabbat. I was nineteen, and had not seen Feigl since about ten years earlier. The first thing she said upon seeing me was, "Oh, you look like them!" Her tone was not very pleasant. I could deduce immediately that my father had not told me some important bit of family business. I played along, ignoring her nasty intonations, and tried to get her to talk about her early life in Eastern Europe. It was like pulling teeth. When I wrote to my father demanding an explanation for her unfriendliness, he wrote back that Feigl had been raised in a village, and had come to Brest-Litovsk to stay in his family's home in order to try to arrange a marriage. She had walked into the home of four beautiful, intelligent, and lively cousins, and simply could not compete. It is not hard to imagine her frustration and depression, and it is typical of Litvaks to have very long memories. So she took out some of her venom on me now, but once I knew the story, I could deal with her. We ended up friends. Having no children of her own, she devoted her life to her husbands and to the community.

The pogroms continued all week long, and in the end one Jew organized a legion—an independent defensive group of 300 men stepping forward in the name of God and Torah. They began to chase the Grigorians, who were on the other side of the Dnieper River, in a suburb. The Grigorians thought they were being attacked by the Bolsheviks and fled, and in this way the city was emptied of these thieves. At least twenty men had been killed when they finally left, and this was a mote of dust compared to the huge numbers of Jews killed in other cities. It helped that the rich people of our city bribed them to let more of us survive.

After a few weeks my health gradually returned, but I was not as before for some time. The good news of my recovery reached my parents, and the joy was great. My sister Peshke and my brother-in-law Rav Moshe Reuven also had typhus [Spanish flu], *and my good news worked on them like health-giving, refreshing nectar.*

After I recovered from my illness, I slowly returned to normal. There was a housing problem for the yeshiva students, because it was difficult to match two or three "appropriate" boys to share space with each other and a host family. Part of the director's job was to make good matches: a more educated boy, strong in his religious identity, could be placed with a weaker boy, less well-grounded in musar, so that the strong would rein in the weak by his behavior and influence him with his way of life. I was matched with Yitzhak of Kelm, a student who had spent most of his life on yeshiva benches and was well-versed in its life while strong and sharp in his knowledge. In the inn we did not live well, and each of us lived our independent life. I did not pay attention to whether I lived properly or not, for I thought I was fine. I did not recognize his [ultimately negative] character traits because I thought that all was proper.

*In the yeshiva, after the Grigory pogroms, learning re-
turned to normal. I observed life in this yeshiva closely, and
recognized a very significant difference between this yeshiva
and the others in which I had learned. Outward appearance
and cleanliness, beauty, the attention paid to particulars of
presentation, the preventing of belching, the pressing of the
crease of the trousers, the folded decoration of the handker-
chief, the food preparation—the sense that food should be
tasty and fresh—all of this was in stark contrast to the fear of
batlanut and the attitude of laughter and ridicule for all things
beautiful as exteriorities and wastes of time and focus from
the soul that I knew from the musar I had learned in the earlier
yeshivas. This contrast awoke a huge doubt in me and a lack
of comprehension as to how to react to this new situation.*

*The lectures of the spiritual supervisor—the Alter, they
called him—were difficult for me. This man was a great scholar.
His face was witness to this fact, for under his thick eyebrows
was hidden deep Torah knowledge. He was much respected
in the yeshiva, and his looks alone put fear into the students,
but also respect. His discussions were full of content and
wisdom. One recognized from them that this man understood
life from the perspective of religion and musar tradition and
knew their philosophy. He used various examples to express
this, and they were always on target, but he spoke very softly,
on purpose, so that the students had to listen hard and ended
up crowded together like fish in a barrel. Then he would speak*

more and more slowly, word by word, to make comprehension more difficult. That is why I could not understand his lectures, and only after much trial and error did I begin to grasp them. This is my summary of them.

Man is composed of two basic parts: the rational mind, the divine part, that which gives him the title "Man," and the part taken from the ground—the body, similar to an animal and beast. There is a constant battle between the "human" and the "non-human" parts, and man's task is to ensure that the human prevails. A man is forbidden to separate the two parts and distance the two, to prevent meeting with the ugly and bad, but must do the opposite: bring a clash between the sacred and the profane and aid in the success of the former over the latter. The beauty of man must win.

His words were mixed in with items from the Talmud as well as from worldly wisdom. He would pronounce the names of scholars with a tone of respect. "Thus would say Aristo," he would begin. I interrupted and asked this question: "If man is a higher being, with a superior task in this world, why was he given ugly body parts that bring about filth, and perform repulsive acts?" He replied, "TEKU" [a traditional statement, an acronym for "Elijah the Prophet will answer in the days of Messiah" that indicates the answer to a philosophical question is not known—Ed.]. *Once the great Aristotle, he told us, was found doing "repulsive work." His students asked him, "Why is a philosopher doing this work?" Aristotle replied, "When I do this I am not Aristotle."*

In the yeshiva, thanks to the strict supervision of the Alter, our behavior was religious and kosher. I began to understand the Alter's lectures more and more, despite the difficulty caused by his soft speech. I had not personally met the Alter yet and so he did not really know me, but once there occurred an event that caused me much aggravation and brought me into the Alter's direct and sharp observation.

I went to the house of my relatives and saw there the book Bikkurim. *Because I had little to do at night during the school week, I took the book back to the dormitory with me. I knew nothing about it, and had no idea that this would cause me so much aggravation and indignity, and that the next day news of my reading material would reach the Alter's ears. I never meant "l'hakh'is" (to aggravate)—I simply found interesting stories in the volume and hoped to enjoy them in my leisure time. It seems, however, that a neighbor in the dormitory did not like this book. He knew it was a secular book and so forbidden, for there were stories in it like "Moshe" by Ahad Ha-Am. He reported on me to the Alter. The next day the Alter's messengers came to request that I appear before him. This summons hit me like a thunderbolt; I feared greatly, for I did not know the reason for it. Trembling, I went to him.*

He was a very wise man who recognized a man's inclinations with one look, a look which penetrated the soul and searched out its secrets. His look, now turned on me, terrified me into silence. He began, with soft words, to talk about my sin. *I immediately understood the situation and did not deny that I had read a Hebrew book, but all his efforts to discover who had given it to me were to no avail, for I would never betray the honor of a dead man. This dead man had been a yeshiva student of Knesset Israel, Yakov Zeitchik. He had died before I came to Kremenchug and many had eulogized him. Had I stated that this book was his, as I had found out after beginning it, he would have lost all of his charm and the good name that he had left. He had been a wonderful student, but he also liked secular stories.*

The Alter began to give me musar. *He asked, "Don't you know that anyone with a secular book dismisses Torah study?" He said many other things, telling me that reading this book was like idolatry, for all impurity is in such things. He told me that they removed man from godliness, and a great deal more besides. I stood still and rued my deed and repented. He demanded that I promise him through a handshake that I would never read secular books again, but I refused, saying, "Who knows what the future holds?" In the end, I gave him a handshake promising that I would not read these books as long as I was in his yeshiva. With a heart full of fury at the cause of this—the squealer—for I immediately knew who it was—I left the house of the Alter.*

The news that I had been summoned to the Alter quickly made the rounds of the yeshiva, and soon everyone knew that I had sinned badly. I returned to the dormitory, took the book, and returned it to its place. I quarreled strongly with my neighbor, Yitzhak of Kelm, who I knew had been the one to tell on me. I got little satisfaction out of this, for he simply responded that it was a mitzva to prevent someone from committing such a bad sin. **[In Volozhin Yeshiva, discipline was maintained first through the removal of honors, such as being called to the Torah, then by reducing the student's allowance, then by a slap, and finally by expulsion. In Slobodka, a network of spying was created to deal with discipline, with a confrontation with Rav Finkel coming on the heel of bad reports—Ed.]**

After this incident, I was constantly watched in the yeshiva, with people checking out everything I did and everywhere I went. At night, I would read The Kuzari, with the knowledge of the Alter, for this book was not forbidden.

At that time, there was a student in Yeshivat Knesset Bet Yitzhak by the name of Motke from Brisk. He was short but physically very strong. He was known as an "Ilui," a genius, with excellent capabilities. He considered himself special in that yeshiva. I remember the story that once at a workers' meeting he strongly opposed Burgan, who was known to pray in Yeshivat Knesset Israel. When this tale was told to the Alter, he threw Motke out immediately. Motke was not bothered by the expulsion. He got up and went to a factory to become one of the workers. After some time, Yeshivat Knesset Bet Yitzhak of Slobodka came to Kremenchug, with the Resh Metivta Rav Boruch Dov **[who was later appointed the rav of Kremenchug—Ed.].** When the

Rav saw that the Ilui had left gemara, the knowledge pained him. He sent Motke a conciliatory letter and brought him back to the yeshiva.

I liked this short young man, and another student named Avraham who had studied in Yelizabetgrad in Yeshivat Lida where they also studied secular things, and I began to grow close with them. I found in them people with whom to share my ideas and outlook, which were not yet totally formed, and we became good friends. **[The Lida Yeshiva dealt with the crises of the Haskalah, Zionism, and Hasidism by reforming the yeshiva curriculum and integrating secular studies into it—Ed.]**

The Pogroms of the Denikintzim
(the Whites)

Meanwhile, the Denikintzim conquered the city. Their entry brought even greater fear than the entry of the Grigorians, for they Grigorians were known to be pillagers and had no political agenda, and were not going to stay in the city for long as its rulers. The Denikintzim were totally political—their plan was to conquer the state and rule it. So we knew we could free ourselves from the Grigorians by monetary bribery—and that is why there were relatively few deaths from their attacks. With the Denikintzim, one could not raise the issue of money, for that enflamed them more—they saw it as an insult to their honor as rulers of the city.

Anton Ivanovich Denikin (1872-1947) was a Russian general, who, after the Bolshevik Revolution, became the commander of the anti-Bolshevik army in the south. Driven back by the Bolsheviks in 1920, he resigned. The anti-Bolsheviks were known as the "Whites," and the Bolsheviks were called the "Reds."

Ukraine was one of the battlefronts of the Russian Civil War (1918-1921), which was complicated by the desire of many

Ukrainians for independence. General Grigory fought under Simon Petlyura (1879-1926), the Ukrainian nationalist, against both the Reds and the Whites. Petlyura was accused of not stopping the pogroms, but rather using them to strengthen his base of support among soldiers and peasants, appealing to their antisemitic tendencies.

The entry of the Denikintzim was awful—as soon they came in, shots began flying in town. Life instantly stopped as if everyone had died. All the Jews hid in their holes and the Angel of Death really began to stride through the city. The color of blood painted all....

I remember one evening during those awful days, as the sun's last rays were licking the earth of the fertile and beautiful Ukraine. Instead of the usual peacefulness that comes with the beginning of evening, a great fear filled the void and heavy worry entered our hearts. All the Jews living around our courtyard gathered. We sat—men, women, and children—and I suddenly thought of Bialik's tragic poem "In the City of Death." I began to recite and explain the poem to the others, and sobs broke from all. The floor was wet with tears. For us this poem was not words printed on paper, but real life, and the words rolled from my mouth into an atmosphere of fear of death, showing our weakness in their wake. The scene was tragic not only because it was reality, but because every one of us wrote this poem with his blood. In the middle of the recitation, shots exploded near the house, and with a great deathly scream, we scattered. Many were already dead and badly wounded, fighting death.

The next day I went to my uncle, the Resh Metivta of Yeshivat Shaarei Torah of Kremenchug. A large gathering of Jews met in the courtyard of the big yeshiva, which was enclosed on two sides by iron gates that were locked at night. At the entry of the courtyard there lived a rich Jew, and when the soldiers came and ordered him to open the gate, he replied that he would never open it. Even though they threatened him and said that they would bomb it open and kill everyone within, he did not open it. They tried to break through the gates, but they were very strong, and each time it seemed that they would burst and we would all die, silence fell. After a time, we thought they had left, but then we heard the sound of cannon wheels and we knew that our end was near. After a few explosions, the gate was pierced, and murderers, drunk with blood, burst into the courtyard. At first they shot over our heads, but then the murderous beatings began. We began to run, escorted by bombs and bullets, to the second gate. I saw people, old men and friends, fall here and there. My teacher Rav Shlomo Heiman ha-Pritizi, bent over and fell with "Shma Yisrael" on his lips. We couldn't even recognize each other—it was as if demons were fleeing as death chased them.

We approached the second gate, only to discover soldiers standing there to greet us with whips in their hands. We were cruelly beaten and had nowhere to turn. We were like trapped animals surrounded by hunters. I don't remember how I suddenly noticed a cellar, but when I did I turned aside and stole in through the door. Even though it was totally dark inside, I was able to make out the shapes of people lying still, like shadows, without any breath. Silence reigned in the cellar and everyone was careful not to show a sign of life lest he betray everyone. Thus the night passed. In the morning we began, one by one, to crawl out of our cave, and each went to search for relatives and friends. How many were covered in blood! How many souls had flown heavenward, leaving just their bodies behind!

Though it was quiet by then, the fear of death had not yet passed and remained for many days, while things calmed down and life began to return little by little to some kind of normalcy. The pogroms ended at last.

Some twenty kilometers outside of Kremenchug is the town of Karilov on the banks of the Dneiper River. The two cities are connected by the Dneiper, and travel from one to the other is accomplished by ferry. The Kremenchug yeshiva students settled among the Jewish residents of the village, and a certain bachelor, who the school wished to reward with a proper position, was appointed rav of the village as well as director of the yeshiva in Karilov. The yeshiva was founded by the Alter himself. He gathered all the weakest students of the yeshiva Knesset Yisrael and sent them to Karilov

under the supervision of the Rav Damta and Resh Metivta—
the aforementioned student. This new Resh Metivta was
a superior Torah and musar scholar. Under the supervision
of these two, the yeshiva developed in the musar style, and
the weak students began to grasp the needs of musar and
delve into them.

I remember that in Elul the entire yeshiva came
to Kremenchug, to our yeshiva, to absorb the spiritual
awakening taught by the Alter in his lectures. From the first
day they showed their deep understanding of the material of
his lectures. It was wondrous to me, because in my earlier
acquaintance with these students, they had never understood
the first thing about musar, and now they revealed such deep
understanding and knowledge that they outshone the rest of
us. This development raised the value of the Karilov yeshiva
in my eyes and led me to feeling a bond with it. Upon my
request, the Alter—who had never fully trusted me since I had
caught his attention by reading secular books—agreed to send
me to Karilov, for there I would be strengthened in my studies.
His additional reasoning, however, was that there I would
constantly be under the supervision of the Resh Metivta, and
the teachers could more scrupulously oversee my life than
the Alter could, for there were fewer students there. I did not
object to this, for I saw the high level of the Karilov yeshiva
and realized that I could raise the level of my studies more
quickly there than in Kremenchug. I desired to delve more

and more deeply into Talmud and musar—*and it was not the location that counted but the content. My goal was to master the studies.*

In the home of my uncle, Rav Eliezer Yitzhak, director of Yeshivat Sha'arei Torah of Kremenchug, my relatives opposed this idea for a simple reason: they feared the pogroms and did not want me to be alone, far from them. But nonetheless, the plan was quickly put into action.

After Succot, the Denikintzim left the city, but before leaving they attacked once more, leaving many bloody sacrifices. These pogroms were not as violent as the first, because by this time the evil-doers had simply become a band of murderers, focused more on money than actual killings. This new set of pogroms lasted half a week. Then the Denikintzim left and the Bolsheviks entered. As soon as the switch occurred, the town began to feel freer and more secure than when any of the other groups had entered. The Bolsheviks took great care not to touch the Jews. I remember that when a Russian commissar passed a soldier torturing a Jew on the street, without any discussion he aimed his pistol and shot the soldier dead, and then put on his chest a note with the details of why he had shot him. As a result of this security inside and outside, I felt prepared, and packed my things and headed on the road to Karilov.

Karilov
(December 1919)

I came to the river's edge and found that even though it was Chanuka, the ice was not yet covering the entire river. As we arrived, a fierce wind began to blow. None of the oarsmen wanted to accept the task of taking us to Karilov. Eventually we found one Christian who wanted to go, and after each of us paid a dear price for the trip we sat down in the craft, which started on its way. The view of the river was fearsome: the strong wind molded the smooth water into moving and scudding mountains and valleys. It seemed that the awful sea storm was endless, covering heaven from one end to the other. It is insane that in the face of such danger, people still go out to sail and become objects in the hands of the horrible rising and descending waves. The shadow of ruefulness stole into our hearts for not having heeded the voices of those who had warned us not to travel during such a storm. The boat was far from the river's edge, and we were in the power of the waves that carried us wherever they wanted. The boat did not sail, but was, rather, carried from hill to valley and from valley to heights. It fell into the depths and up to heaven....

The boat held many Gentiles and a few Jews. I looked at the faces of the Jews and saw hidden fear, the fear of possible death that I had seen during the pogroms—fear of the raised sword. I saw their lips moving, probably in recitations of prayers and Psalms—perhaps, even, vidui (the customary confession before death). I could not bear to contemplate the dangerous situation, and all I could do when the boat plunged and reared was hold on with all my might to its sides so as not to fall overboard. I saw numerous fearsome scenes before my eyes. In my imagination, the hidden depths were no longer hidden: I saw exactly what you do not want to think of appearing in my brain like flashes of lightening. These were horrible sufferings, the sufferings of a man whose vision flutters between life and death. I had never suffered so, and therefore these moments are indelibly inscribed in my memory.

The trip took a long time because of the storm. We looked ahead and around us to see if there was any dot of land. When we saw in the distance the outline of houses, it was as though life was breathed into us. We grew closer to this vision as we approached the fork in the river as it splits into two streams. The distance around it was wide.* Because of the rushing water, it was impossible to navigate the river at this point, and the boatman began to take us to the shore: we did not want to endanger ourselves even more by entering such roiling waters.

---

* It is unclear what is meant by this description.

Karilov (December 1919)

The boatman got the boat, by then nearly broken, away from the crushing currents and made for the head of the larger of the two rivers. There we all got out and stood on the land to wait until he would return for us in a stronger boat. We suffered greatly while waiting, for it was cold and we were completely wet after the crossing. With watchful eyes we awaited his return, until finally we saw a small black dot approaching. At first we couldn't believe our eyes, but as it neared we saw that it really was a new boat, which he had taken from the other side of the Dnieper.

He demanded a special fee from the Jews in the boat, for transporting us to the city despite the fact that we had already paid him more than enough. When we refused, he said that he would not take us at all, so we were forced to pay him every last cent of his new fee. As was typical in this sort of situation, from his fellow Christians he did not take a thing. We boarded the new boat, and after enduring more dangers, we arrived finally to our objective. After we descended onto solid ground, I began searching for the house of the Rav. Finding it, I entered at last, broken and shaken from the terrifying voyage.

The Karilov Chapter

The Karilov yeshiva was unlike those in other cities. Its economic situation was very weak because of its poor surroundings, which could not support it. The students, therefore, did not receive any monetary stipends, and so had to be permanently placed at the tables of others—a custom which had long since been discarded by the other higher yeshivas. The custom's reputation was abominable in the eyes of the students, but in this yeshiva it was acceptable, and each of us spent a day or a few days or weeks or even months with this or that rich man. I did not in any way want to agree to this custom—I not only did not want to, but absolutely refused to, even if I was left with no means of support and without even a penny to my name. Even knowing that I would suffer greatly, I refused to give in. The battle, and inner battle I could not reveal to others, was great. I felt that if I went to eat at another's table I would kill all my feelings of independent pride—I could not do it. I fought for and with my stomach. The battle expressed itself, and I felt true hunger. I did not eat cooked food, and my diet of dry bread and water badly affected me. And it was not just the hunger pangs that hurt me but also my sleeping arrangements, for I also fulfilled "on the earth you shall sleep" in all its details. I came to experience the true life of "the sons of the poor from whose mouth emerges Torah." The battle with my stomach lasted a while, until it defeated me and I fainted. My insides became sick, and I could no longer digest food.

After my illness, when my strength returned, I was persuaded to eat lunch each day with the town's richest man.

If the physical life was terrible, the spiritual life was satisfactory, and it was this that gave me strength to attain my primary goal: to succeed in Talmud and musar.

The Resh Metivta, Rav Yechezkel of Trestin, was totally and completely dedicated to the yeshiva. Day and night he was immersed in the labor of teaching and clarification. His method of teaching was very pleasant and geared to the students' development. His discussions, in which all participated, were very interesting. We debated and discussed in depth each topic in all its minutiae. His manner of teaching did not situate him as a lecturer and us as the passive listeners. Instead, we all participated on equal terms as we sought out the main reason for a legal decision.

I can still picture in my mind's eye the discussions on Shabbat evenings—not in the yeshiva, but in the dark dormitory, which housed most of the students. We had no furniture, so we all sat on the floor, one leaning his arm on the edge of a trunk, another leaning his head on the shoulder of a friend. We were all ears as we listened to Rav Yechezkel and each other intently. The room was totally dark, and we could not make out any faces. It was a sweet, comradely, and still darkness that enveloped the room, with only black stains and black shadows spreading over the walls, one shadow swallowing another, and one stain crawling over another. In the deep silence one could hear only the voice of Rav Yechezkel explaining the essence and uniqueness of Judaism. He showed us how the entire Torah revolves around one basic element: "and you shall live with them." It did not, as he pointed out, teach that "you shall die by them." It is a Torah of life, and worthy to each soul. He compared and contrasted our commandments with the laws of other nations. He might say, for example, that in the Gospels it is written, "It is better not to marry your entire life, but if you must, and you marry, you may never divorce her!" He would evince astonishment: how difficult a law! On the contrary, he taught, man must live, and for that he was born and created, but he must live like a man. That is a basic condition, and man must not give in to what is ugly in him: "not for chaos he was created, but for Shabbat." A man is not to go childless, but rather should follow the commandment of "Be fruitful and multiply." If his wife does not please him, "he shall give her a get (divorce)." Our Torah is not like their scriptures, for we are not told to distance ourselves from life, but are on the contrary meant to enter life—though we must take care and remember always morals and ethics.

Another topic Rav Yechezkel spoke of was anger. It is written in the Gospels that "Man is forbidden from anger." There is the story there of a sea captain traveling in a ship, and the sailors bothered him and did not let him rest—and yet he did not punish them. No! Man may be angry, and is meant to be so if people besmirch his manly honor and diminish his godly nature. Rav Yechezkel brought dozens of examples like this, and in his "educational language" he sent off sparks, cut and dissected, and drew and painted the image of Jewish ethics as the ultimate form, above all the others. His words always hit their targets, and his answers settled the doubts and questions which constantly buzz in the mind and heart. He came close to all of us, became one of us in his simplicity and innocence, and his immediacy impelled me to ask for an answer to the question that constantly pained me: the question of "pain to living creatures." I told him of the various opinions that I wrestled with in seeking an answer in musar. I told him of Tolstoy's opinion that men should eat plants alone, and never animals, and he responded to me that being eaten is not a burden to the animals, for they were created with the purpose of giving man the possibility of repairing the defect of the soul of the animal by making the blessing of ritual slaughter. Everything in this world was created for the good and enrichment of the Jew. The animal is to provide food for man and to provide men a means of praising God. Therefore, a Jew is not only permitted to slaughter the animal, but it is a mitzva to eat its meat, if he does so with the proper blessing and intent—the intent to repair the defect. It is forbidden to the ordinary people to eat meat any other way. Rav Yechezkel attacked Tolstoy and other Gentile searchers for righteousness, saying, "Pay attention to the suffering of people and the poor, and don't worry about animals who do not comprehend what is done to them!" This answer persuaded me, and the issue was set to rest at last.

I dedicated myself to my studies, and constantly reminded myself that the desire to develop intellectually was the reason for my being there, even though our physical situation was far from satisfying. The yeshiva atmosphere strongly influenced me, and I was strict and Orthodox. I remember that one time when I came to the rich man's house for Shabbat lunch, I found a guest there smoking a cigarette. I said nothing, but with a loud slam of the door I stormed out of the house. For many days I did not want to return, but my hosts kept coming to me and apologizing and promising it would never happen again. So I returned to eat. I was so pious then!

The Kotzerim Pogrom (1920)

Not far from Karilov is a primeval forest which no man has yet explored completely. There are sections that have not changed since Creation, and that no man has even seen. Various wild animals are to be found there, in the impenetrable darkness. It is a terrifying place. Strange cries of animals of prey rise up, and forest birds chirp harshly, bemoaning their inability to leave the forest, which serves as a hiding place for a famous band of thieves under the leadership of Kotzer. Kotzer excelled at brigandage and, had done so for many years without any fear of capture. Fear of him exists not only in the local populace but also within the police and army that had not been able to capture or kill him in their many attempts. Like a locust, he would strike from one side, disappear in a second hole, and reappear on a third side. He was like a rat teasing a cat that had come to catch him. He himself did not participate in the attacks and thefts perpetrated by his men, but was instead the leader of his army, which was armed from head to toe with all sorts of weapons and went wherever he sent it. Wherever his men attacked, they left terrible destruction. People were slaughtered, and riches were stolen and hidden in caches between boulders. Their best hunting happened during times of anarchy and unrest, like what Ukraine experienced after that change of rule.

One afternoon, the armed "Kotzerim" burst into the town, took over the government offices, and threw out the Bolsheviks. Their entry was in the manner of thieves, and not that of political rulers, and so, as I mentioned earlier, the results were more horrible. A great fear descended on the town's residents as they learned that the conquerors were the Kotzerim. They knew from that alone that there would be no mercy, and nothing could soften the conquerers' hearts. The pogroms began....

Even though I had already experienced a number of brushes with death, there was a special fear here, as though grey leaden clouds weighed on my soul, overcoming me, choking me.... Horrible sounds came from here and there, the echoes of attacks. The pogroms took on an especially awful shape due to the nature of the town. It was small and we all knew each other, so if one householder was killed by the merciless murderers, we all knew him and were affected.

One memory, which is strong in its generalities and yet cloudy in its details, is of a time that I came face to face with death. The incident is engraved in my heart, and the image of the grave open before me still passes before my eyes. Three armed Kotzerim brigands broke into the yeshiva one afternoon. There were only a few of us students there. One of the brigands, who was drunk, came to me and demanded money, holding his rifle near his chest. Without thinking, I opened my wallet and showed him that it was empty but for three rubles. In his disbelief and drunkenness he loaded the rifle and aimed at my heart. I was frozen in my place out of fear. I lost all feeling. As a result of the pogroms, our physical situation was awful, and we had no means of sustenance. We hadn't eaten nor drunk in some time. The days of eating with the rich had ended because it was dangerous to go outside. We lived on dry bread and salt— and this may be what saved me from death! At the moment that all feeling left me and I could not focus, and before my eyes appeared an open black grave ready to swallow me, my lips instinctively began to move—to say what? I don't remember what I was thinking, but I am positive that what I thought to say was the vidui—the confession that would get me into the next world. I remember everyone crying, and hearing a wailing that reached heaven, though all in my memory is muted as though I was in a deep sleep. The student Levi from the Ukraine stood, holding a piece of black bread sprinkled with salt, and in Russian he begged them for mercy, told them that we were poor, without a penny in our pockets—just look at the black bread and salt that we were living on! I was sure that the heart of even a thief and murderer would melt from our tears, and so it was. One of the brigands began to push the hand of the drunk and prevented him from killing me, but the drunk refused to be dissuaded from firing. The shot echoed amid the walls of the yeshiva, but the bullet hit the ceiling instead of me.

The ceiling shattered into pieces, and smoke and dust filled the room so that one couldn't see anyone else. In this turmoil the brigands and I were hit by debris, my friends told me later, and I fainted; it took some time to awaken me. Broken from this close brush with death, and with the awful economic structure of the town overcoming its spirituality, I decided to leave Karilov and return to Kremenchug.

The road was dangerous, but I felt I had no choice, and so I gathered my things and sat in the wagon, and we carefully left for Kremenchug. It was a difficult trip. The driver's price was so high that I could not afford to sit on the wagon and I had to run on foot after it. The storm sent its white horns [of lightning] and they lit our path. Slowly we moved away from the bloody field, and my spirit began to relax as the hours passed and we went farther away from those who wanted to slaughter us.

After a long trek, I came to Kremenchug exhausted. Yet instead of the peace which I had hoped to find after the horrible pogroms that had shaken me to the core of my being, I found disease rampant in the city's populace. Spanish flu spread like a veritable plague over the city, hitting the already traumatized population.

The Spanish influenza pandemic, lasting from 1918 to 1919, is estimated to have killed between 2.5 and 5 percent of the world's population, or between 50 to 100 million people. It was often misdiagnosed as cholera or typhoid. The majority of the deaths were from bacterial pneumonia, a secondary infection caused by the influenza. An unusual feature of this pandemic is that it killed a disproportionate number of young adults. In Eastern Europe there seems to have been pockets of the disease into 1920—unless the communities simply lumped a group of terrible diseases together, assuming them all to be influenza.

The yeshiva students too fell victims to the disease, and Knesset Israel emptied of people. They were taken to the hospital and filled the beds there. One after another they succumbed, and the yeshiva was closed, for even the directors felt that nothing was normal. Everyone busied himself with visiting the sick and providing them with food and other needs. Because the studies there were stopped, I did not enter Yeshivat Knesset Israel, but instead went to Yeshivat Shaarei Torah, led by my teacher Rav Shlomo of Poritz. But the plague did not pass over this yeshiva either, and it spread quickly, one boy after another succumbing. This was depressing for all, and we each feared catching the fearful illness. We were all in shock as the shadow of death hovered over the yeshiva, and horrified especially by the speed with which the disease spread. Each of us was certain he would catch it. We poured our souls into chanting Psalms in a tearful, sad tone. We all chanted, and cried buckets of tears on the bet midrash floor. Our crying and weeping expressed our desperation as we suffered under the sword of the disease held over our heads after escaping only barely the sword of war. There was fear and deep despair, an inability to find a ray of hope through the black stormy clouds of oncoming death. We felt the anguish of our sick friends and acquaintances, their loneliness—felt the tragedy that their love of Torah had caused them to leave their homes and brought them to battlefields and to a pandemic which in a sense was revenge on the killers who had spilled innocent blood, blood that demanded the revenge the illness took. Those days were horrific, and the night seven times worse. Summer nights in the Ukraine are extraordinarily beautiful, but the shadow of the Angel of Death hovering over its width and length replaced the charm with a taste of death and rotting.

Then a piece of news arrived like a spark of light: Kotzer and his gang had left Karilov, and everything there was back to normal. I quickly packed my things and set out for Karilov. I hoped that there I would finally find peace and could renew my studies once more. But it was not to be: I did not find peace, but illness, even more dangerous and awful, for scarlet fever had come to Karilov.

Who had brought it? Where had it come from? Hadn't I seen enough misery in Kremenchug? Maybe the illness was chasing after me, for it had to infect me and send me to bed, since I had escaped the flu. In Kremenchug there were hospitals to house the sick and provide them with basic medicines; here, however, the yeshiva was turned into a hospital, with beds on the floor and pillows made up of an old, torn coat. And the conditions? Anyone who did not see it could not imagine anything like it! One next to the second, the second next to the third—all the sick lay on the floor in their impurities, with unchanged sheets and without food. High fever ravaged the sick, and they lay like sticks on the earth. If by a miracle some milk appeared, no one knew who to feed first, for we were all thirsty with burning lips, searching for liquid relief. The number of the sick grew, and I was counted among them. We ourselves were the doctors, asking each other if the sweating had passed, for that was a crucial phase of the disease. I changed completely— when I recovered slowly, I was unrecognizable. I tried to go out for a bit, leaning on a stick, and the caretaker of the yeshiva asked me my name—she did not recognize me even vaguely.

Meanwhile the town had a new conqueror—Babenko and his army, who were not as terrible as their predecessors, though their hands were not entirely innocent of blood. If they did not often murder, they pillaged five times more than the others.

After the disease of scarlet fever [or perhaps Spanish flu; he was unclear on the distinction—Ed.] had passed, and the yeshiva had begun to recover, we were hit with malaria. I succumbed to this too, but recovered. What had I done to deserve such suffering? It remains an unsolved mystery. Meanwhile, the news arrived that Yeshivat Knesset Yisrael was preparing to leave Russia and requested that our yeshiva join in. Learning had been weak all summer because of the diseases. I was broken from my own tribulations and had no energy to wander alone. And so we joined the Slobodka Yeshiva Knesset Israel and we left Karilov.

Kovna

When I left Karilov I had in mind to go via Bobruisk even though I had already been notified that my parents had left Bobruisk and were back in Brisk in Poland. It was in order to meet the girl, Sima Brishensky, for whom I felt uneasiness. I planned to meet her in Bobruisk.

We arrived in Kremenchug after an awful trip, and I went to bid farewell to my grandmother Rotke and my relatives. The Resh Metivta of Karilov Yeshiva, Rav Yechezkel, was there. It was a very warm farewell, and it's incised in my memory. I didn't kiss my grandmother's face—because of my musar ideas, which forbade it—but her last words to me were very sad, expressing that she had no hope of seeing me again. "I have nothing to give to you as a present for you to remember me forever," she said. I didn't understand the full impact of those words, for I did not then know that they are the type of words said by a person on the edge of the grave, who wants to leave something in the world of the living. Rav Yehezkel kissed me, and I left with the idea of going to Bobruisk.

The trip was full of pitfalls. The travel of the Children of Israel to the land of Israel was via a desert infested with *snakes and scorpions; our path was even worse! It excelled in its many curves and the dangers that accompanied us without end. Rail travel was forbidden, and if you did take a train, your travel was either illegal or through bribery. We had to sneak from one station to the next and from one car to the next in order to hide from the conductor and the various inspectors who walked and searched the cars for illegal people. And what would happen to someone who was found? They would take him out of the carriage and give him hard work that would break his body. This I know from personal experience, for during our trip, I more than once had to work at various jobs at various stations—I chopped wood, hauled water, and such. I was not accustomed to such work, but I did the tasks despite their difficulty. After we completed the work, they would sent us away and we would continue on our way, with no confidence that this would not happen at the next station—and even with foreknowledge that it would.*

The journey in general was very difficult and, worse, dangerous. There was a constant danger that our progress would be halted, that we'd be forced to do hard labor for an unknown length of time. And the same game continued—hiding and rushing from one car to the next, fearful of coming face to face with those searching for us, and ending up in jail. One awful event that forced me to rethink the plan of my trip occurred at the Zhlovin station. I was traveling with my friend, the son of the rav of Shklov. At that station they took us off the train and brought us to jail. They began to cross-examine us, scrutinizing our documents, etc. I have never figured out why I was favored, why I was able to talk my way out to relative freedome while they put my friend in prison. I decided to travel via Borislav, so I could turn aside to Shklov to tell Rav Damtah about his son's imprisonment so that he could hurry to save him from his tormentors. I was exhausted by my ordeal and fell asleep on the train there. While I had asked my neighbor in the cabin to awaken me at the Shklov station, he did not do so, and when I awoke I was already far away from Shklov. I felt horrible that my best friend remained in such a terrible situation, and that all his hopes of relying on me were for nought. The one light in his future went out, and it was all my fault for I was not bringing him rescue—and also because I was the one who had chosen this route, due to my hope of meeting with Sima in Bobruisk. The idea of my responsibility troubled me. I felt guilt, but what could I do now? When I got off at Borisov I wrote a letter to the Rav of Shklov, his father, and thus found some satisfaction for my soul and my worries.

In these difficult conditions I continued on my way and arrived at Minsk, and from there continued to Volozhin. There I met up with my old friends. Many had already left our traditional world for the "evil culture" (the secular world) and were gymnasium students, and others were on the threshold of the yeshiva and prepared to joyfully start a new chapter of *their lives outside of it. Others had become even more religious and had closed themselves into the world of halakha without allowing even a ray of external life to penetrate. These last influenced me. The fact that hundreds of students not only escaped the new streams that penetrated the yeshiva but even delved deeper into the Torah and were thus fortified showed me* musar *heskel. It served as a guide to me and strengthened in me the desire to learn and reach higher and higher.*

From Volozhin I set out for Vilna, which had been conquered by the Lithuanians. The route was as difficult as the crossing of the Red Sea. Passing through the Bolshevik border was like penetrating a battleground during war, especially when those Bolsheviks did not want to be bribed and did not allow you to cross the border. Finally, after various ploys and tricks, we **[It is unclear who his companions were at this point; they may have been simply people he met along the way—Ed.]** *stole across via the woods and took deep roundabout paths that no human had walked on since Creation. Only we, those urged on by attacks, dared to endanger ourselves with such a route.*

After a night of deep, indescribable fear, we arrived at Vilna, then the capital of Lithuania. Here I began to think about continuing to Slobodka, but that city could not be reached easily: each traveler was obliged to pass a test in the consulate, a test about the geography of Kovna and its surroundings. For a few days I prepared for the exam, which I fortunately passed, and then I received permission to travel. I came to Kovna and Slobodka.

The yeshiva was then in a state of upheaval. Students were beginning to arrive from here and there. Each told of his sufferings and adventures, recounting how many times the Angel of Death passed over his head, how many times he was miraculously saved from certain death. I too began to empty my "poisonous cup," but I did not know that a new chapter of suffering was beginning, and it would be even worse than the others. If the cup had not been filled before, here it would be.

The Slobodka Chapter

After all my trials and travails, I arrived at Kovna. **[Slobodka Yeshiva was located in a suburb of Kovna—Ed.]** *The external appearance of the city, the planning of it all, which differed so from the cities of Russia where I'd lived before, influenced me greatly. It was clear that the horrors of the war had not reached here to leave their signs of destruction. Life was normal, and there was economic activity similar to what there had been in our pre-war life.*

Now I began to feel greatly lacking—a sense that accompanied me wherever I went. I began to look askance at my torn clothing and to feel how much sneering they caused and how I was viewed as inferior because of them. The rich environment, the externalities, the ironed shirts and suits that went back and forth, all forced me to pay attention to my poverty. I felt awful, depressed, and broken. In the yeshiva too, the economic situation was good. At that time, the donations were beginning to flow to Eastern European lands and institutions such as the yeshiva received many hundreds of dollars in support. This money invigorated the yeshiva, strengthening hope, and contributing to our belief in support which added vigor to religious life, our study of Torah and its rich sources. The good economic situation manifested itself in many ways, including in the clothing of the yeshiva students, which was for the most part elegant and classy, but the influx of dollars was not as recognizable in the lives of the students as it was in the lives of the heads of the various yeshivas. They began to dress in "peer ve-khavod" (elegance) and began to live good lives. The yeshiva students too began to absorb from the riches of the yeshiva, and aside from the food—which was pretty good—they bought respectable clothing.

But I was the exception. I don't know if this was because of past sins—certainly the administrators still suspected me of going on the evil path, and were concerned that I had not repaired my deeds nor changed for the good—but whatever the reason, I suffered greatly. It did not even enter my mind to have a new suit sewn for me, and my food was poor and meager, and given to me with a bad attitude, not with the same generosity with which it was given to the others. My appearance was awful. I wore torn clothing and patches in that bitter cold winter. In addition to the physical suffering, the spiritual suffering was great. I endured terrible anguish due to the special attitude I received from those who boldly separated me from the others, causing an internal pain that was hard to express to others, because it was borne of the depth of the feelings of a helpless innocent man who has fallen into a pit and cannot defend himself.... I could not go to the directors *and complain and cry and beg, for it would not help, and also because it would be matter of spiritual defiance, so I suffered greatly from lack of the most basic means needed by a man, and suffered depression from the musar that also oppressed me. I felt a coldness around me, and received strange up-and-down looks from the director, the Alter. The motive behind this was to force me to come and beg in front of them, and to apologize, and to try through good deeds to find favor in their eyes, but the result was the opposite. "As he suffers, so he shall grow and spread." The more they oppressed me, the stronger my determination grew. I decided never to give in to their desires. I did not do anything purposely to arouse them, for I had not yet reached that stage, and I was involved with the musar ideas so it was alien to me. Rather, I threw myself into my studies. I turned away from secular ideas and my many troubles and I diligently studied, to find healing for my wounds and my broken heart.*

At that time, there was a young student in the yeshiva from Jerusalem, and he was an Ilui, with wonderful ability—possessed of a wide grasp, understanding, and an exceptional memory. He was honored in the yeshiva and considered its star. The directors had great hopes for him, and there was in fact much to anticipate from him. He was worthy of being a "new star" in the heaven of Jewish genius, for he was still young—only nineteen years old—and his future was assured. I grew close to this student, and together we decided to study

Masekhet Yevamot. He had a good nature, and I found in him a good friend. In bad times—and when wasn't it bad?—I opened my bitter heart to him. But the yeshiva directors, with their "higher politics," decided to ruin this friendship. As soon as our learning partnership was discovered by the Resh Metivta, Rav Moshe, son of the Alter, he summoned me and attacked me: How could I dare to steal the hour of rest from the Ilui like this! Isn't every moment of his time more precious than pearls?

In truth, these things had a scent of righteousness and fear of heaven in them. In fact, because they thought I was a certain, disagreeable "type" as far as sticking to the path of musar was concerned, they didn't trust me to learn in partnership with the Yerushalmi lest I ensnare him with secularist ideas, and also because they were envious that this genius and I were friends. They used various pressures to convince us both. They feared that I would use our friendship in my war with them, so they used every means to cut the thread of friendship that was beginning to embroider us together. Me they warned with loud commands not to come into the space of the Yerushalmi genius, and him they "advised" not to come near me, for I might spoil him. He had to obey, since he depended on the directors for his daily needs. And so our partnership and our friendship—that one bright note in my dark path—ended, and I returned to the darkness of my woes.

Life was indeed difficult. The winter that year was harsh, and my clothing did not cover my entire body. The freezing wind penetrated to my skin, but this was nothing compared to my internal suffering—my feelings of loneliness and otherness. How much it pained me to see the other students living well, dressed in the latest styles! And I—naked and without—what did I do to deserve this? What was my major sin? I could not find an answer, but bad people wanted bad things for me.

Still, the sun did not hide forever behind black clouds: a saving angel came to let in some rays of sunlight. This time the light took the form of my friendship with the student Shmuel Dov of Vilna. This student was also a great scholar, with excellent capabilities—if not quite so remarkable as the Yerushalmi. Unlike the Yerushalmi, he was strong in musar and had passed many personal trials, which were by now part of him, as he had won numerous battles. In short, this was a tested student, and so the yeshiva directors, upon being informed of our partnership, not only did not forbid it, but on the contrary were satisfied, for they hoped that his musar approach would influence me for the better. We set times during the day to study—in addition to the regular twelve-hour seder and the musar classes, we learned at night after the classes were over, and especially at four in the morning. Every day I would go at that early hour, the time when all around is still silent except for the the rooster crowing the news of the new day, and when the morning star is just beginning to rise and spread its clear light over the world still wrapped in the veil of night. Despite the awful cold which pierced the bare skin like needles I would stand at the appointed time under the window shutter of Shmuel-Dov and awaken him from his sweet morning sleep to come to worship. When my voice reached his ear he quickly arose to run to fulfill his holy task. This was in fact dangerous for me, for my feet were bare and I was constantly in danger of getting sick, but I went anyway, day after day. It was an indescribable feeling, a spark from the spirit of the "Matmid" who sacrificed himself on the altar of Torah—the only reward of his life. **[This is a reference to the poem by Chaim Nachman Bialik, "Ha-Matmid."—Ed.]**

Our partnership in learning gave me much satisfaction and was my only consolation in my loneliness. Thus two to three months passed until the evil inclination came and stole from me even this enjoyment. Because my economic situation was so bad and I was penniless, I could not rent, like the other students had, a decent place to live. However, by a miracle I had found a narrow corner in the room of a poor harness maker who was married and had children. The room was four by four [meters] and in one corner I found my place of rest for a tiny sum of money per month. The lack of cleanliness was not to be believed—one could sink in the filth. Still, there was one redeeming feature to the dark trap which had no word in a lexicon, for room=food=sleep=work: the room served all purposes, and the knocking of the harness maker getting up to work in the unreal early morning awoke me and got me on my feet to awaken my friend Shmuel-Dov for the gemara lesson. Aside from this, there were other outstanding characteristics of the room. First, at night, when the time for sleep came, a division appeared in the room like a tree growing from the ground, with one part of the room reserved specifically for my bedroom. The color of the walls was impossible to determine, for they were covered with ash and spiderwebs, black like the Angel of Death and gray from the smoke that rose in the soft air. This was the home of a "ghetto" Jew, burdened with many children, the type of home that the greatest artist, with the strongest imagination, could not possibly paint.

It was no wonder, then, that after two months in the house I got sick, mainly due to my lack of clothing. I caught a cold, and that became pneumonia. It is difficult to describe the horrible conditions in which I was sick. This time the yeshiva concerned itself, and sent me a doctor and good food. They paid me back, but not enough, for the very people who caused my pains were worried that I would die. Giving against one's will: that is the path of the evil one. They called the best doctor of the city for me, Dr. Berger. He tried very hard to heal me and in the end succeeded. Slowly I regained my strength. As a result of my illness, my studies with Shmuel-Dov stopped. He showed great concern during my illness, and came to help me. He became even more dear to me, and "my soul was bound to his." **[This is a reference to the tale of David and Jonathan—Ed.]**

Those were the days of the great awakening in America as a result of the horrible rumors that reached there about the catastrophic situation in which the majority of the Jews of Eastern Europe found themselves after the difficult war and subsequent pogroms. News spread, telling of the thousands of orphans whose parents had been slaughtered, and who remained without any means of survival. Rumors of poor widows and ordinary Jews left without even clothing awoke the hearts of our brother Jews in America; they were suddenly motivated to help the refugees of Europe, and especially those relatives who had not been heard from during the long years of the war, the war that had closed off America as though it was behind the Great Wall of China. Even Lithuanian Jews' relatives in America became concerned, and there was a search for relatives and neighbors, with the goal of extending help to them. The yeshiva students sent announcements to The Forward, *the only American newspaper that reached Europe, and it began attempting to find relatives. I, too, lacking all means, and knowing that I had two brothers in America, sent an announcement to* The Forward *searching for them. After a short time, I received a response from one of them, who was fortuitously an editor for* The Forward. *Even more remarkably, as I later found out, he was the very editor who handled all inquiries of this nature.*

My brother's letter was received by the mashgiach of Yeshivat Slobodka, who read it. I was sent for and told that a letter had arrived, with a photograph ... and money. The messenger told me this with quiet satisfaction, and seemed to want to suck my marrow **[drive him crazy—Ed.]** *with his choice of timing—he told me during the seder (study period)! Naturally, I wanted to immediately run and see what had arrived for me, but I was not allowed to leave in the middle of the gemara lecture. Every moment seemed like forever to me, but finally the class ended and I ran to the home of the Alter. So slowly— as if to stretch my soul—they took out the letter, photograph, and money. I shouted from joy and did not heed their musar of "Look! Watch! What brothers you have! Leftists!"*

I did not answer a thing, and I left full of hope for the future. I felt strong. I now had a source of sustenance. I would not have to rely on the yeshiva, and I could continue with my battle of refusal to succumb to the politics that were haughtily aimed at trampling the weak. I would now not be afraid, for the money would protect me.... The feeling that I was not forsaken strengthened me, and I whistled with joy. I immediately ordered a new suit; I left the house of the leather-worker and moved into the house of Shmuel-Dov from Vilna as a roommate. I began to breathe more freely—and life was good!

Now that things eased up for me, I opened my eyes and began to look around. The barrier was gone, and I could observe people outside the four walls of the yeshiva. I looked at the larger world, which was a thousand times greater than what I already knew. I no longer felt totally bound by the knowledge that the yeshiva was looking at my religious behavior, so during my free time, I began to visit the city on the other side of the river—Kovna. One time the young man Alyashuv met me and took an interest in me, asking if I was interested in Haskalah. When I nodded agreement, he advised me to go to the Mapu library. I didn't stop to think about what drew me there, aside from the thought that I could find newspapers there, especially the American Forward in which I could read my brother's articles, and my intellectual dissatisfaction. In addition to books by Mapu itself—there was a complete collection—I also found there many other books and newspapers. Slowly a world was revealed to me, a world that wasn't completely new to me, but was entirely different from that of the Talmud and the musar books I was accustomed to studying.

I was not instantly overwhelmed by this new material, nor was I overly enthusiastic, but I am sure that this was when I crossed over a threshold and something within me changed. The signs of an inevitable spiritual revolution began to show in me, but I can't say with certainty whether without the external push from the directors of the yeshiva I would have changed my life so drastically. For the yeshiva directors had set up a spy group made up of students whose job it was to check up on the virtues of every yeshiva student. If something suspicious arose, they went and squealed to the "higher *authorities," which then meted out punishments, whether harsh or light.*

This was how the spies caught me: one of my [female] acquaintances came from Russia and extended her hand to me in greeting. **[Men and women were expected not to touch each other—Ed.]** *This immediately came to the ears of the Alter, and so the intrigues developed. The evil tongue wagged, the lies grew, and the hand knew how to weave the net to trap me. The spies gathered material, and the tales grew from day to day.*

Spring had arrived in full force, and spring in Kovna was uniquely lovely. What special magic lay in the tall mountains, the valleys, and the river! Nature is gorgeous there. It was no wonder that the writer A. Mapu could sit atop these mountains and see in his imagination the land of the deer—Israel—during its blooming, with such nature in front of his eyes—Israel, with its eternal sun and magical blue skies and green grass. The beauty of nature influenced me, too, and I felt drawn to the outskirts of the city, to the fields, mountains, and river. When my feet touched the earth outside the city and I raised my eyes up and saw the fertile land and the sky in all its shadings, I felt that they were close to my soul and body. All of the shattered elements of my life that had been crushing me, especially the spiritual pressure of the walls of the yeshiva, fell away and I stood up straight again. To experience this feeling, I would rush to the river during my free hours to bathe, to enjoy the mountain views, and to have the ability to straighten up from the constant bending over the pages of the gemara. I breathed deeply and felt that I was inhaling reinvigorating air—sometimes I even napped in the quiet, which was in a way hard to describe like a soft song.

Often, during spring afternoons, I left the city and went to swim in the river, but spying eyes reached even there and a report of my undignified behavior was made to the Alter. It also happened that I was found lying on the grass reading a newspaper and secular books. And so the vicious intrigues and rumors against me grew until they came to a peak. This time, it was the library that snared me. I would visit the library without fear, for I told myself that any yeshiva student who would come here was sinning like me, and so would reveal nothing. I was careful, but once when I descended the stairs of the library I met the granddaughter of the Alter! She was allowed to visit the library, for that was how girls were educated among the religious—despite the fear that it would serve as a window to assimilation. My heart fell when I saw her, and I thought, "if I am lost, I am lost." [This is a quotation from the Book of Esther, ch.4, verse 16—Ed.] *Still, I hoped that she would not tell, but I was wrong—and my fear was well grounded.*

A week later, two weeks before Shavuot, a command arrived: I was called to Rav Avraham (Grodzinski) of Warsaw, the son-in-law of the Mashgiach of our yeshiva. He was a big baal musar and one of the spiritual and physical leaders of the yeshiva. With my heart pounding, I went to him. My eyes saw a face full of wrinkles, each attesting to holiness and fear of God, and my ears heard his serious words: "In our view your father is a Gaon in Torah, and we know well his desire to educate you to be a Jew like him. We cannot accept the responsibility for your education, for we do not find in you the reassurance that you will walk in the path of musar and fear of God. Our advice is this: go home to your parents and enter the supervision of your father, who will take care of your future!"

How sanctimoniously he said this, all of it "in the name of holiness," pretending that he was acting of the purest intentions when in reality all of this was a political ploy. When they saw that every means of persecuting me had failed, and that my material situation was now firm and good, there was no other route than to expel me from the yeshiva, lest I serve as a bad example to others.

The expulsion was announced to me in a tone not of advice but of final decision, and so I knew not to respond. I admit openly that I was a bit fearful, but only a bit: the fence of my world had already possessed holes, but now I felt it toppled completely. I was given a push to leave the world of the yeshiva and find another—a better one for me, with more spiritual satisfaction. One thing I knew in the core of my being was that rays of new light were shining into my room from other worlds, worlds which I had read about in books—the world of the present, a rich world whose ideas were pulling down the earlier ideas that had been based only on the Torah and the place of man in the world. They took into account real life and living nature.

Internal struggles—first in the mind and then in the heart—commenced; a bomb destroyed the fortress I had built especially around my idea of man's role in the world. I had always been taught that man's fate was not in this world, which was merely a dark corridor to the next, but I now knew that the corridor was not ugly but beautiful and reasonable. I had questions that required answers.

It seems to me that when the old passes with nothing new to fill it, the emptiness of the heart grows. There are times when the stink of rotting roses from your old dark world pushes you out and tells you, "Go while your soul is still in you, and flee from here, from the darkness to the light! Open your heart and eyes to what is around you—see the purity of science, drink from it and slake your thirst and feel your being. Know that you are alive, a man among men, a creature among creatures. There is even a place for musar and "higher politics."

I remembered the attitude the men of the yeshiva had had during my time of poverty and depression. Their behavior had marked them and musar itself with an indelible stain that could not be washed away or forgiven. That war between the old that was going to destroy itself or be destroyed and the new streams was not only within me but within the hearts of many students who read secular books in secret, and I was not the only one ready to leave the yeshiva.

In the yeshiva itself, learning was weak. The summer season approached, and the directors prepared to leave for their summer homes, some outside and some inside the borders of Poland and Russia. There was no future for me in the yeshiva, so I made a decision: I would go home to Brisk. This did not solve the question "Le-an—Where to [ultimately]?" that stood before me in all its sharpness, but I knew that leaving the yeshiva was a cardinal event in my life. With the chains of its rules broken, I could leave the world of the "old" and rotten to enter into a new world—how good this new world would be I did not consider; it was enough that I was escaping not just from a place but from its content and reality. What would fill its place? I did not know, but my heart told me that it would be good. As an act of revenge, I demanded of the yeshiva's directors a large sum of money to cover my expenses and debts. Since they had made such a show of acting for my own good, they had no choice, and gave me what I demanded.

I went to bid the Alter farewell. I remember that he kissed me on my forehead in front of the students as a proof that he had no personal animosity to me but acted for my sake. He left me with a warning: the end of this relationship must not serve to distance me from the path I had been on until now, for that path was the only straight one in life.

I left Slobodka and the world of the "wings of God" and traveled to Vilna. There I arranged to cross the border, and arrived home for Shavuot to the warmth of my parents, who received me with exclamations of joy after not having seen me for such a long time. The house was full of happiness.

Written: 22/IV/26

So ends my father's memoir, on April 22, 1926, but of course his story was still near its beginning.

What Came Next

Q. How did you get back to your parents?

A. I was lucky: in Vilna I caught the last train that belonged
   to Poland, because later on there was a war between
   Poland and Lithuania. Later on you couldn't go. And
   I arrived in Brisk.

   My parents did not expect me. It was an unusual
   reunion, because they had received a letter from Rav
   Aharon Kotler (from Kletzk) praising me that I had found
   an answer to the Kivieaiger's (Rav Akiva Eiger, 1761-1837)
   kushia [question]. To answer on this topic, you have to
   be very sharp. And because of this he wrote to Father,
   "Please send him right away [to Kletzk]!" But I told
   Father that he had other motives—he wanted me to be
   a groom for his sister-in-law, Rav Isser Zalman's daughter.
   When I had studied there before, in Slutzk, she had kept
   an eye on me—I wasn't blind. But I was too young—I was
   sixteen or seventeen.

   I said to my father: "Father, you had very bad
   experiences with two sons, that because you only gave
   them an education in gemara they went to the other

extreme and became Bundists, and Communists. I don't want to have this experience. The only thing I want is this: I MUST know secular studies."

Q. Was your father upset?

My father told me that my grandfather's curiosity about the world was insatiable. However, he did not read secular books to satisfy this curiosity. What he did instead was question the multitude of visitors who passed through his study about a wide variety of topics. Sometimes he would then entertain his children with what he had heard. For example, he was fascinated with Inuit life and how the Inuit tribes hunted whales. He could not get over the fact that whales could hold their breaths under water for as long as they did. I can just picture the wonder this must have caused in my father's imagination, since he remembered these stories decades after his father's death well enough to repeat them to me.

A. No. He said, "Yes, I can solve the problem with one letter." The Meitchiter Illui is rosh yeshiva in the Takhkemoni of Bialystock, and in his yeshiva one learns secular studies. And so it was. I took the letter and traveled to Bialystok, and even though they did not want to accept anyone, and I had no money, the Meitchiter said that I should be given a very hard test, and I passed it. I was not interested in his brilliant classes—he was the

145

best rebbe I ever had—I wanted only secular studies.
I completed the four levels of high school, including in
mathematical studies. I had a teacher who at one time
was a yeshiva man who instilled in me the love for the
Hebrew language I learned Polish and Latin and history.
(I have two photos of the Meitchiter).

My father told me on another occasion a slightly different
version of the story: that when he was nineteen he wanted to go to
Bialystock to study in the new school called Takhkemoni, run by
Dr. Balaban. The school, as it is described above, incorporated not
only the traditional curriculum, but also in-depth study of Bible
and modern Hebrew, along with the latest literature being written
in Hebrew by Zionist writers like Chaim Nachman Bialik. My
grandfather, faced with this 1920s dilemma, made the decision to
allow my father to go to Bialystock, and then Warsaw, and gave him
his blessing. He had suffered terribly from the lifestyle of his two
older sons, who had become socialists and dropped every aspect
of traditional Judaism. After a couple of years in Takhkemoni,
my father's idealism became such that he came back to Brest-
Litovsk to ask his father's permission to go to Palestine. This time
his plan was not to attend a yeshiva or a Hebrew academy, but
to study in the newly created Hebrew University of Jerusalem.
Again, my grandfather weighed his options. There is no doubt in
my mind that the fact that my father's contemporary, Joseph Dov
Ber Soloveitchik, was studying at the University of Berlin played

a role in the positive attitude that my grandfather eventually adopted. Both young men already had strong traditional yeshiva education but were highly motivated to obtain secular educations as well. Their paths were to crisscross over the decades.

It was my luck that I arrived during his last year—he was soon to leave for America, where he would be part of Yeshivat Rav Yitzhak Elchanan. My graduation was therefore in question. It was then that Dr. Friedman came, for Prof. Balaban could not—he was the director of Takhkemoni in Warsaw. Professor Balaban was the only person involved with the yeshiva who had a university degree in Jewish history. So he sent Dr. Friedman. He gave us a very difficult examination at the end of this year, and of all those who took it, only two passed: I and one other—a very poor young man from Bialystok. Later, when Bialystok fell to the Bolsheviks, he became the secretary of the Communists. Today [at the time of the interview—Ed.] he is one of the richest men in the world, and lives in South Africa, where he owns mines.

R Moshe Soloveitchik was then the rosh yeshiva in Takhkemoni in Warsaw. There had been a whole fuss over this: Rav Haim Soloveitchik, his father, had written to Father that he should influence him not to teach in Takhkemoni. I don't want to talk about it. [My father did not have the dates quite right here, as Rav Haim died in

1917 and Takhkemoni didn't open until 1920. However, the negotiations for setting up the school were going on during the war—Ed.]

I studied there for one year, in the highest class—there are seven classes in a gymnasium—and there was a huge disagreement (makhloket) then. The other student [who came with me from Bialystok] was being tested by Rav Moshe, and they discussed a *ma'amar hazal* on King David. Prof. Balaban made fun of it. Rav Moshe wanted an apology, but Balaban was not afraid of men like Rav Moshe, and would not apologize. So there was a *makhloket*, and Rav Moshe resigned. That is why I did not get *smicha*. But I did get a beautiful letter of recommendatiion from Balaban, for when I came to Eretz Israel in 1926. The other years I studied in Takhkemoni.

I had no money, and I did not go home. Father used to send me some money and I did not have to pay for the dormitory. I was very happy at Takhkemoni. While there, I went to hear the Philharmonic for the first time—I was dumbstruck and became an ardent music lover. And I went to the theater for the first time and was astonished there as well. Warsaw was a real city!

My aunts got busy sewing shirts for my father for his trip to Palestine, and he had trousers made by the local tailor. He packed his books, his photographs, and his few pieces of clothing. His

sisters gave him some money, as they had been working for years as nurses. He promised to pay them back. His ticket was paid for by the Palestinian Jewish agency for immigration (the Jewish Agency did not come into existence until 1929), as he was allotted one of the prize places in the British quota system for 1926. It was a very exciting time for him, yet also a frightening one, as he feared that he might never see his family again. But the lure was too strong, and at twenty-three, he was just the right age for such a big move. He felt he had no future in Poland and did not want to study in a European university.

Rishon Le-Zion, 1926

Agricultural farm, 1926

Dead Sea trip, 1927

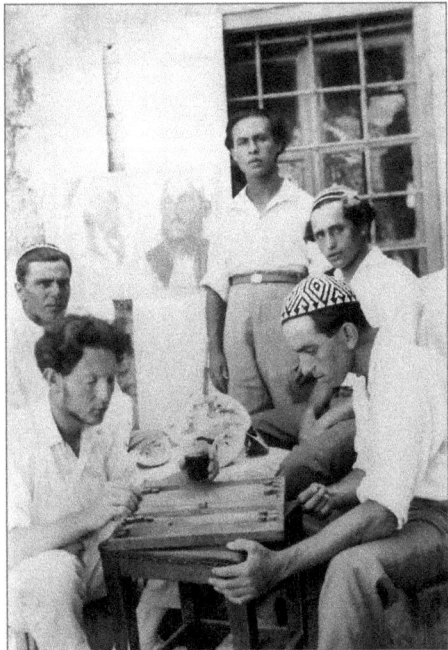

Bezalel, 1928

Moshe Aron Reguer,
Bezalel, Jerusalem,
1928

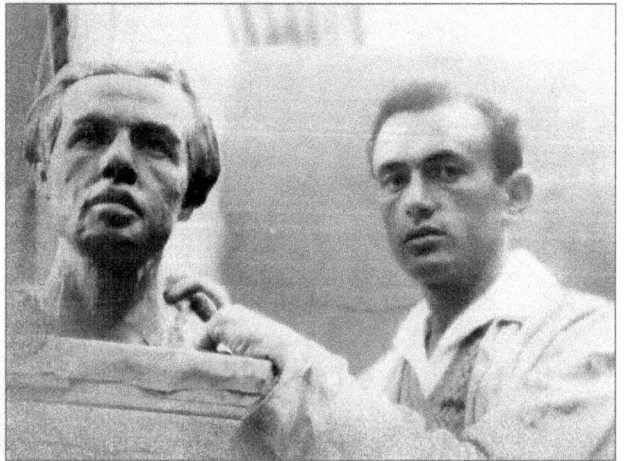

Bezalel, 1928

Hebrew University
Mt. Scopus Construction,
1929

Bezalel, 1928

Part II

MANDATORY PALESTINE/

THE UNITED STATES

INTRODUCTION TO PART II

Throughout the millennia of Jewish history, there has always been an emotional and religious connection to the Land of Israel. Diaspora Jews face Jerusalem when praying, and many of the prayers contain verses describing the longing to return there and be an independent people again. Holidays are connected to Israel's agricultural cycle, and even life cycle events reflect the desire to return to Zion. Over the centuries people went there to die, bodies were sent there for burial, and Holy Land earth was exported to go into Diaspora Jewish coffins.

During the nineteenth century a new form of Zionism came into existence, in line with the new ideas about nationalism. The new thinkers were activists, finished with the passive attitude of waiting for the Messiah to lead the way, and political Zionism was born.

While the pogroms of 1881 and the May Laws of 1882 were a major encouragement to the Jews of Eastern Europe to emigrate to the Americas, they also precipitated a small movement of Jews to Ottoman-controlled Eretz Israel, in what is now known as the "First 'Aliya." This was followed over twenty years later by the "Second 'Aliya," which involved many more people. The two demographic movements differed greatly, in part because during those two decades, the World Zionist Organization was born, led by Dr. Theodore Herzl. Herzl's ideology was optimistic and activist. In keeping with the mindset of his time, he worked to persuade a Western power to grant a charter for the new Jewish colony and protect it as a favored trading partner. At the same time, he set about organizing world Jewry to prepare: to purchase land, invest in the colony, and encourage Jews to move there.

By the time of the outbreak of World War I, there were about 85,000 Jews living in the land of Israel, inhabiting a number of agricultural settlements and building a new city named Tel Aviv. They were also speaking a revived form of Hebrew. Most of the newcomers were socialists.

With the defeat of the Ottoman Turks, along with their allies the Germans and the Austro-Hungarians, decisions had to be made regarding how to deal with their provinces and colonies. The newly created League of Nations invented the "mandate" system, mandating control over areas that were viewed as backward to either France or Britain, whose task it was to teach them how to rule themselves, western-style. The result for Palestine was the British Mandate.

The task of the British Colonial Office in Palestine was made difficult when the Arabs refused to cooperate. The Jews, realizing that they would do better to create their own reality than to rely on the British, set up a quasi-government of their own, thereby learning how to run a state. The mandate document approved by the League of Nations included an article setting up a Jewish agency to cooperate with the British and other articles promising to help in land sales and immigration.

However, as early as 1922, the British hedged their pro-Zionist promises by passing a series of new policy papers, known as White Papers. The 1922 Churchill White Paper, while aimed mainly at setting up a Jewish-Arab legislative body, in fact only ended up introducing the concept of economic absorptive capacity. Immigrants could enter Palestine as long as there were jobs. The British set the numbers for visas, and the Jewish organizations decided who would actually get the visas.

This was how matters looked when my father applied for a visa in 1925/26. The visas were usually given to young adults who knew Hebrew, had trained on an agricultural farm in eastern Europe, and were active Zionists. My father fit the bill on all counts. However, even though his visa lists him as a carpenter, he—and the Zionists in Poland who granted him the visa—knew that he would not be working on an agricultural settlement but would instead be attending the newly-opened Hebrew University.

When the quasi-government of the Yishuv, the Jewish settlement of Mandated Palestine, started functioning, one of its intentions was to set up an educational system spanning "kindergarten"—a new concept at the time—through a university, including teacher training institutions.

The idea for the Hebrew University of Jerusalem predated the Mandate period, but its cornerstone was laid on Mount Scopus in 1918. It was not until 1925 that instruction began. The first three institutes that were opened were in Jewish studies, microbiology, and chemistry. The intention was to develop as a center of Jewish tradition within the framework of the humanities, as well as to become a center of research in the natural sciences. Judah L. Magnes, an American scholar, became chancellor (later president) of the university, and was in charge of the humanities. The funds to run the institution were raised by world Jewry. The language of instruction was Hebrew, and students came from the Yishuv and from abroad.

My father was part of the Jewish studies program, but he also took courses in oriental studies and general humanities. Late in his time there, when he knew that he would be leaving for America in 1929, after three years of study, he went to see Magnes about getting a formal transcript to bring with him. The response was a resounding "no," for the students were meant to enjoy learning for its own sake. So he worked around Magnes, and came to Columbia University with signed attestations from his professors, which were evaluated and accepted by Professor Salo Baron.

There were few scholarships available to Hebrew University students in the 1920s, as fundraising was geared more toward hiring professors and constructing buildings. To support himself, my father got a job working once a week in construction on the Mount Scopus campus, and I have photographs showing him at work. The Zionist ideology encouraged self-labor—Jews doing the physical work on the Yishuv—and my father participated in it.

However, he could not live on the wages of this once-a-week construction job, and so, utilizing the Hebrew language skills he had carefully cultivated first on his own, and then at Takhkemoni, and then again as he prepared for the move, he landed a job as secretary to Boris Schatz, the founder and director of the Bezalel Academy in Jerusalem. Schatz, a Bulgarian Jewish sculptor, founded the academy in 1906, with the intention of creating Jewish- themed craft industries in the Yishuv as well as serving as a cultural center in general. World War I almost destroyed the academy, but Schatz revived it and became a talented fundraiser. His language of communication with the Diaspora was

Hebrew, but his Hebrew was deeply imperfect, and my father's job was to put Schatz's clumsy and grammatically incorrect correspondence into beautiful literary form.

How my father got this position is unknown, and I must resort to guesswork. It seems likely that it was a result of his serving as a model for various artists in the academy. He was unusually sensitive to art, and probably went to investigate the Bezalel Academy for himself. He had a beautifully-shaped head, and it seems that the artists, upon seeing him, asked to use him to depict the "new Jew" or the "halutz" (pioneer). As evidence for this, I can note that when he came to America, he brought with him some of the Jewish-themed bronze plaques that made "Bazalel" so popular, a series of photographs of the busts sculpted based on his head, and two outstanding watercolors painted by Thadeus Rychter and his wife.

My father said, later in his life, that Boris Schatz was a dictator and very unkind to the students. He got some small revenge, during his last days at work before leaving for America, by sending out letters written exactly how Schatz had dictated them, errors and all.

The Eretz Israel Chapter

To get to Palestine, my father and the other young men and women in his organized trip took the train south from Poland. When they got to Trieste, they boarded a freighter, which stopped at all of the small ports along the Adriatic Sea and the Eastern Mediterranean until it reached Jaffa port. There small boats came out to meet the ship, and the new arrivals were rowed to shore, where they could view the new city of Tel Aviv rising from the sand dunes north of Jaffa. From there it was a train ride to Jerusalem.

I came to Israel in 1926, and there I suffered from hunger, for I only had one day each week of work—Thursdays— and that work was physical labor, for twenty piastres a day. I could not rent a room, so I used to sneak into a *shul* after the evening *davening*. My life was very bitter. Until I wrote a letter to my brother in America, my situation was awful. Things were better once I got to America. My brother arranged it by going to the Meitchiter Illui, who went to Dr. Bernard Revel, who got me a visa. And the other students at the university envied me.

Q. What made you decide in 1926 to go to Palestine?

A. The *smicha* in Takhkemoni was impossible, so I lost my
student status and I would have had to go into the army.
I did not particularly want to serve in the Polish army—
my God, so much antisemitism! And to endanger myself
for Poland?! So I gave up my Polish citizenship and
received a visa for Eretz Israel.

Q. Did you go through the Jewish Agency?

A. I went through the Zionist *halutzim* (pioneers) of Brisk.
They gave me a certificate immediately. They were
astounded that the son of Rav Simcha Zelig would go to
work in Eretz Israel.

Q. So each time your father's name helped?

A. Everywhere. With the secular authorities and with the
religious.

Q. You left from Brest-Litovsk, so you were home for a while?

A. I had to come to Brisk. He was beloved by all, by
religious and non-religious people alike. . **[In 1937 his
father's seventieth birthday was written about in the
newspapers, and these were very secular papers—Ed.]**
They wrote about how he would answer questions even
for a poor woman who came with a chicken and claimed
there was no gall bladder—he found it.

**This story may deserve more explanation. My grandfather
labored to find answers to *halakhic* questions that kept in**

mind the individual who asked the question. The incident my father refers to occurred one Friday, when a woman came running frantically to their house waving a newly killed chicken.

"Reb Simcha Zelig, there is no gall bladder! There is no gall bladder, so the chicken is *treif*!"

My grandfather looked at the woman, knowing that if the chicken was judged non-kosher due to its poor health, there would be no meat for Shabbat—she was too poor to buy another one. He said, "Give me the chicken." Knowing full well the anatomy of fowl, my grandfather lifted the raw and bloody bird to his mouth and licked the proper area. Making a face because of the taste, and then spitting out anything that was on his tongue, he declared that there had been a gall bladder, but it had somehow disappeared. The chicken was kosher.

The woman left happily, rushing home to soak and salt it for the proper amount of time, and then to boil it for soup and the main course for her poor family.

The other people present when this occurred marveled at both the decision and the compassion behind it. His reputation spread all over Eastern Europe and beyond.

Q. Was your mother all right at that time?

A. When I left for Eretz Israel, she was fine. I told her that if she cried, I would be very upset. So she didn't—she cried later—all night.

We still have family photographs taken in 1937 that show my grandmother after her stroke. When I was very little, I thought that a certain person in the images was an old man, and a scary one at that. No, my father told me, it was my namesake, ten years after the stroke which had paralyzed half of her body. Sorke spent the last eleven years of her life in constant pain. Care for her devolved on my Aunt Feigl, since she was living in the apartment anyway. But this was not the only aspect of Feigl's life that was burdensome—her marriage was as well, as shall be discussed.

As my grandfather aged, he had some health problems. One of them was that he could not drink alcohol. He debated with himself over this issue in connection with the four cups of wine traditionally drunk for the Pesach *seder*, and although he usually was stringent about such rules for himself, for this he heeded the doctor's warning and drank grape juice. Decades later and worlds apart, my father developed diabetes, and my husband squeezed fresh grapes just before I lit the holiday candles, so that the sugar content in the grape juice would not be a health hazard for him. Was my grandfather also a late-life diabetic? I doubt it, or he would not have been able to drink the overly sweet grape juice at all.

Q How many people lived at your house at this point?

A. Feigl and Esther came with Mother [to the train]. Feigl and Esther were married. Chaim Ber [Gulewski] was a little boy.

Q. Could they already tell that there was something wrong
with his sister?

A. In 1937 I went to Warsaw to Dr. Korchak, and asked him
if anything could be done for her. I would send money
from America to pay him. "It's impossible to help her,"
he said. **[It had already been made clear, in 1926,
that she was retarded—Ed.]** She recognized me—I sat
from afar and followed the instructions I was given for
how to act with her, and she recognized me. She was
pretty when she was little. She was killed with Janusz
Korchak: the Nazis wanted to save him, but Korchak
said, "No, I go with my children!" **[Dr. Janusz Korchak
(1878-1942), was a Polish-Jewish educator and
pediatrician with a practice in Warsaw—Ed.]**

My father told me that my aunt Feigl's marriage was not
a good one. Her first child, a girl, was a disappointment because
the first grandchild in traditional Jewish homes should be
a boy. But it became even worse: later stories claimed that
during the birthing, the baby, later named Chana, suffered
some brain damage. It is certainly possible that this happened.
It is also possible that she was simply mentally deficient. Be
that as it may, there was no sympathy for Feigl coming from
her husband. On top of all of the disappointment and tension
surrounding this birth, my grandmother suffered the stroke that
left her half paralyzed. Feigl, still living in her parents' house,

found herself mothering a retarded child and nursing an ailing mother.

A few years later, Feigl gave birth to a male child, Chaim Ber. Everyone celebrated, but her marriage remained shaky. It reached such a point that my grandfather had to interfere and tell his son-in-law, Moshe Reuven, that Feigl wanted a divorce— the marriage was not salvageable. You can imagine the grief this caused everyone concerned.

My father told me that after years of begging for a divorce, my aunt finally prevailed. On the day they were to complete the religious divorce, known as a *get*, she started out for the Bet Din, or Jewish court, down one street, with Moshe Reuven walking down a parallel street a block away. She could see him as they came closer to the Bet Din, block after block, and imagined her new life without him. But as they actually approached the building where the rabbis had convened to sit as a court of divorce, he changed his mind, turned around, and returned to the house. He had decided that he would rather stay in an unworkable marriage than give up his status as son-in-law of Simcha Zelig.

My father never forgave him. This experience may be part of the reason why my grandfather started working intensively on the issue of modern-day *Agunot* (women chained to dead marriages by husbands who refuse to divorce them), or rather recalcitrant husbands. Unfortunately, all of his work was destroyed by the Nazis. Who knows what could have come out of his legal decision-making on this topic?

With no sons at home, one daughter in Warsaw, one daughter in America, and one daughter on the other side of town, it was only natural that my grandfather paid special attention to his only grandson living in the same house as him. Chaim Ber glowed in this attention and did not want to go away from home to a yeshiva. There were enough yeshivot in and around Brest-Litovsk for him.

When my father came to visit Brisk in 1937, when Chaim Ber was already fourteen, the antagonism between the two was born. The teenager resented the arrival of the American uncle, a rabbi and teacher at Yeshiva University, newly married, and seemingly rich. My father looked at his nephew as an upstart, and resented him as the son of the despised Moshe Reuven who would not free his sister Feigl. The fact that Chaim Ber also looked like Moshe Reuven, his father, did not help. Their mutual dislike was an undercurrent in their relationship all of their lives.

Q. So from 1926 to 1929 you lived in Palestine. I know the famous story of the shower and how you had your clothes stolen, the ones your sisters made with loving care, and you ended up with *shmattes*. I have the impression, however, that even so you were an extremely good-looking man.

A. I was! I suffered hunger, but very nice girls from very nice families tried to go out with me. I couldn't take them out, because I didn't have any money. One girl was very beautiful, and she invited me to go to Jericho. I said I had

no money—I even had big holes in the soles of my shoes.
But I went with her, and her family had a vehicle.

Q. What did you do there?

A. We toured the archeological dig. There is a museum
named after the head, Meyer, who was married
to a Christian. She was very rich, but it was a scandal!
And one of my teachers was in love with the girl who
had invited me, and very jealous that she paid attention
to me and not to him. He wanted to marry her, but she
was not interested in him. She was a beautiful blond.
I liked her very much, but I was just too poor. She
married a very nice young man. She advised me
to work as a book dealer, but I am such a terrible
businessman.

Q. Who were your teachers at Hebrew University?

A. I had many. I studied Greek and Latin with Schwabe—
I had already studied Latin in Takhkemoni. We had to
learn Virgil by heart, and I can still recite a large part of it.
I had Epstein for Talmud—it was very hard to get into his
class because you had to know two *sedarim*, not *masekhtot*.
But I had learned in yeshivot, so I was accepted.

**My father told very few stories of his three years in Israel,
but he kept a small stash of photographs from that time. I guess
he felt he should not share the things he did during that time with
a daughter. The photographs, however, speak for themselves.**

There is a shot of him on the agricultural settlement of Rishon Le-Zion, posing in a *kaffiye*, with dozens of other young people around him. This was probably his first stop after arriving at the Jaffa port, with his documentation stating that he was a carpenter.

The other photographs show him on various trips to tourist areas, again alongside others of his own age. We see him posing in shorts and polo shirts, but more often in open-necked shirts and slacks. The others in the photographs are probably his Hebrew University classmates.

Some interesting shots are of Bezalel School sculptors posing next to busts of my father's head. He has a number of shots of the artist Thaddeus Rychter and his wife. He also posed formally in front of the ornate doors of the Bezalel institute.

One of his stories was about his once-a-week job as a construction worker on Mount Scopus, helping to build Hebrew University. There is a wonderful photograph of him and his construction crew doing just that. This was part of the Zionist ideal of self-labor—i.e., the Jews of the Yishuv would do all of the physical labor they needed done, and would not hire Arabs for such work.

The photographers were excellent, and the faces of the young people are very expressive. They are the dreamers and the idealists, the ones who left their homes in Eastern Europe for the land of their dreams, ready to face its hardships. They are mostly male, but here and there you can see a young woman with a fiercely determined face. When my father succumbed to the constant pangs of hunger and left for America, many of his friends gave him photographs of themselves inscribed in Hebrew with wishes for his return to "our land of Israel." One of them wrote that she hoped he did not wait to return until he was ready to be buried on Mount Olives.

One thing that remained with my father for the rest of his life was his knowledge of the Hebrew songs he had learned while in Israel. He would put us to bed singing a Hebrew lullaby— *Shikhvi ve-radmi bat li yakira*, "Lie down and go to sleep, my darling daughter"—and dream of the land where our ancestors were free, a land of milk and honey. He would sing for us the poetry of Rahel Blaustein, set to music: *Ma yafim ha-lailot be-chna'an*—"How beautiful are the nights of Canaan." And, his absolute favorite, *Kineret sheli*. We had nightly singing sessions, with my father's deep voice and clear pronunciation imprinting those songs on my brain forever.

Back in Brest-Litovsk, his sisters were making important life decisions. Esther, the prettiest and smartest of them, met a tall handsome man, Zalman Chary, who was one of the most eligible bachelors in the city. He was not a yeshiva man, but rather a worldly man of business who was already one of the richest men in Poland-Lithuania. His fortune had been made in connection with the expansion of railroads into Poland-Lithuania.

Esther knew that Zalman was not exactly what her father wanted for her, but at least he was traditional and had great respect for my grandfather. When he courted my aunt, unlike my uncle by marriage Moshe Reuven, he was interested in the woman and not in her *yichus*. Moshe Reuven married my grandfather's daughter; Zalman, however, married Esther. My grandfather agreed to the match and the wedding took place. Beautiful Esther moved into the richer part of town, into her own house, where she and her husband settled down to raise a family of three daughters. The photographs taken of them reflect their wealth, and the fact that they had a huge dog showed how far my uncle and aunt had moved from the ghetto Jew's fear of such animals.

Throughout all their years of separation, Aunt Esther wrote constantly to my father, whether he was in Palestine, or, after 1929, in the United States. Her newsy letters are a treasure trove of information about the family and the situation in Brest-Litovsk in the mid- to late 1930s. Her handwriting evinces education, as does her choice of vocabulary, and the letters are written only in Yiddish. There are very few letters from my Aunt Feigl, and even fewer from the youngest aunt, Peshke. Peshke probably was least comfortable of all of them in written Yiddish, as can be interpreted from both her handwriting and her writing style in her few letters. Her preferred language was Polish, reflecting the huge age difference between herself and her three older sisters. As for my Aunt Golde, she emigrated to the United States as soon as her two older brothers sent for her. She had rejected every suitor who had come to her, had become a socialist, and was independent enough not to want to be tied down in a traditional marriage. In the 1930s she did marry, in the United States, but hers was an "American marriage." She and my uncle Morris Ginsburg had one daughter, my cousin Charne.

Peshke was always rebellious and couldn't wait to get out of the house. No longer a practicing Jew, she refused to marry via a *shiduch*, and certainly was not interested in a yeshiva man. She wanted to find her own way in life, following her socialist beliefs. She probably had help from her other sisters in achieving her escape. She ended up in Warsaw, and at one of her political meetings, she met her future husband. Unfortunately, he was married to someone else at the time. He felt the same way about her as she did about him, though, and after he left his wife, the two married. They had one child, a boy, before Hitler invaded and destroyed them all.

My grandparents probably kept thinking that they had done something wrong that had caused so many of their children to choose different lifestyles, but they hadn't. The cause for these changes was the time in which they were living—it was the new ideas, and, for the daughters, the lack of a solid Jewish education. When you are a thinking person, as most Litvaks are, gender does not determine who gets the brains, and questioning is part of us. If the tools for finding answers are not provided within the tradition, thinking people will look outside of the tradition. My uncles in particular were under the spell of Marx and Lenin, and the desires to both help the oppressed and rid the world of antisemitism. They were young and impressionable, and the end result of their work was so disillusioning that they left Eastern Europe for America. My grandparents, as religious people, saw the actions of their children as a burden placed on them to prove their devotion to God.

Q. Did you get *smicha* from your father?

A. I did, but didn't use it. I got *smicha* from Yeshiva University, and that one I used. I understood that otherwise my *smicha* would be suspect, because a father is a father.

Q. Did you involve yourself with learning at all when you were in Palestine?

A. No. But Epstein's class was Talmud. The rest were secular. Joseph Klausner was a teacher. The best professor was David Yellin, who was a friend of the students and who knew that we were hungry. Almost every Shabbat he invited us to his house.

Q. Aren't your old classmates big shots now?

A. All of them are. Prof. Lieberman, one of the deputy mayors—I had a strange experience with him at the funeral of Prof. Sasson. He gave a yell to me: "We are the last two alive!" I answered, "What do you want, that we should lie down in the grave?" Everyone laughed.

Another one, a known archaeologist, met me in Mossad Bialik and said: "Shalom Reguer!" After fifty

Smicha of MAR by SZR, attested to by R. Binyaimin Aronowitz, 1937/8 years! But I forgot his name. He had gone to live with the Beduins to study Arabic. His books about the Beduin are the best. Everyone else is dead.

Q. Did you miss Israel when you came to America?

A. I had a bad experience. When I went to America in 1929, the Arabs killed a number of my friends from Slobodka Yeshiva in Hebron. I went to the consul to get permission to return to fight the Arabs, but the English Consul would not give me a visa.

The New York Chapter

My father came to the United States during the summer of 1929. He had his university credits from Hebrew University evaluated by Professor Salo Baron at Columbia University, and went on to use them at Yeshiva University.

Q. Did you miss Israel?

A. I missed it a lot. I didn't have any choice about leaving, though, because I was starving. I knew that someday I would go back and not suffer hunger. It took forty-five years.

Q. You kept in contact with your parents by writing?

A. Of course. I have all the letters.

During my life I had experiences that I never expected. I purposely chose to travel by boat for thirty-one days from Jaffa to Providence, Rhode Island. My brother paid $175 for a first-class ticket for me. Right after I arrived and met my brother , this same boat, the *Asia*, was hired to bring 700 Arabs to Mecca—and it sank. I paid my brother back for the ticket, of course. In fact, he needed money, so I paid him more. I took care of this debt before I got married.

My father told me about his trip to America on the *Asia* on a number of occasions. One of the places where it stopped for a couple of days was Naples, Italy. My father got all dressed up to visit the city, and was astonished that uniformed men kept saluting him. He figured that this was simply what Italians do as a greeting, so he saluted back. It was not until he returned to the ship and described his experience that he learned about Mussolini's "Black Shirts." It seems that he was wearing the beautiful black shirt sewn by his sisters, and looked very Italian with his dark Litvak skin, and so the soldiers saluted him as one of their own.

The United States' open-door policy toward immigrants changed right after World War I. It became harder and harder to get visas, especially for people in Eastern Europe. The enormous immigration of Eastern European Jews to the United States, which had started in 1881/1882, ground to a halt after Congress imposed strict new laws in 1920.

With the new rules in place, not only did families have to fill out forms guaranteeing monetary support for their immigrating family members, but—for students in particular—institutional support had to be guaranteed as well. It also was an open secret that immigrant visas were given much more readily to people from Great Britain and France than to eastern Europeans.

My father, of course, already had the support of his brother Haim, and the institutional support of Yeshiva University, in part through the activities of the Meitchiter Illui, Rabbi Polachek, who had probably received a letter from my grandfather asking for help. The evidence for this is a letter sent in 1928 by Rabbi Zerach Epstein, Rosh Yeshiva of Torath Haim Yeshiva in Jerusalem, to Rabbi Bernard Revel. (The letter can now be found in the Yeshiva University archives.) In the letter he attests to having been contacted by my grandfather and asked to write to Rabbi Revel about my father's qualities. He also noted that he was asked to please help my father to obtain a student visa. There is an additional letter written by the president of the faculty of the Rabbi Isaac Elchanan Theological Seminary in August 1928, asking the American consul in Palestine to grant my father a visa.

The last piece of the puzzle fell into place when my father received his Mandatory Palestine passport, for this made him officially British, despite the statement in the passport that had had no guaranteed right to come to Great Britain. He received the passport in Jerusalem on February 4, 1929, and on February 14 he obtained a visa from the American consul in Jerusalem. He then bought his one-way ticket to Providence, Rhode Island, on the *Asia*, leaving April 12, with stops in Turkey, Greece, and Italy. My uncle had advised him not to come via Ellis Island, where he would be subject to a long wait, considering how many immigrants came in that way. "Buy a first class ticket, disembark at Providence, and just walk through passport control," he said, and that is exactly what my father did. His brother met him in Providence, and they traveled together to New York City, catching up after the decades in which they hadn't seen each other—almost the entirety of my father's life. A new chapter was about to begin.

Q. How did you meet Mummy?

A. Rabbi Kupietsky had invited me for Shavuot. There I met my future wife. She saw how I was laughing, and it made a bad impression on her. But after, when we went onto the roof to talk, I saw that she was for me. At the same time I was being offered, by a very well-connected family, a dowry of $40,000 to marry another woman. I turned it down—your mother came just in time. Her outward appearance made a strong impression; she was full of cleverness and good nature. Two years we went out, and we came to know each other's secrets. We decided to get married. It was a very poor wedding, but I have no complaints. I loved my father-in-law, and as it was he had to borrow money for the wedding. "Don't look at the cover but what is inside," he told me later, in his last words to me before he died. But Mother gave his things away—I had wanted his watch. A yeshiva *bochur* dreams of getting a golden watch and a *Shas* from his father-in-law. When I saw how poor my father-in-law was, I bought my own *Shas* and my own watch. And my bride didn't wear a white dress, because they had no money to buy one.

My mother's version of the story was slightly different.

My father told me in greater detail about how he met my mother. He had been in the United States about four years and was living in Manhattan, renting a room in a large Upper West Side apartment belonging to a widow by the name of Mrs. Epstein. As often as possible, he would spend Shabbat in Borough Park, as that was where the young single people gathered and socialized. One Shabbat he met a young woman, Anne Shabasson, who had travelled from Montreal to see her newly married sister, Celia Greenberg. He and my mother liked each other from the start, but it was many years before he asked her to marry him, because he didn't earn enough money to support a family. He was teaching in Etz Hayim Yeshiva in Brooklyn, in Yeshiva University High School for Boys in Washington Heights, and at Teachers' Institute for Women in midtown Manhattan, while continuing with his own graduate studies at Yeshiva University.

Before he proposed at last, he wrote home to his father to get his blessing. The problem was that my mother was from Mozhitzer Hasidic background and even in the 1930s there remained an anti-Hasidic attitude among Mitnagdim, as my father's family was. My father was on tenterhooks waiting for a reply.

My father awaited the response from his father, which arrived some weeks after he wrote. My grandfather, who was so respected among the Hasidim of Brest-Litovsk that they would come to shake his hand every Shabbat, laid my father's fears to rest, responding that as long as she was a *shomeret mitzvot*—an observant Jew—and a proper *bat-Yisrael*—daughter of Israel—the marriage should go ahead and would have his blessing.

My parents were married on Friday, April 3, 1936, in Montreal. It was three days before Pesach. The holiday was the only vacation time that my father had, so my maternal grandmother and all of the women of the family and community worked together to provide a wedding feast. Then everything had to be cleaned for Pesach, and they combined *Sheva B'rakhot*, the traditional daily celebration during the first week of married life, with the holiday.

My mother could not wait to adopt the customs of Mitnagdut, as her personal experiences with Hasidim and Hasidism were not that good. My father's general attitude to women within Judaism and the education of women was eye-opening for her. The family they began used all my father's customs—the only custom that my father adopted from his father-in-law was the wearing of a silver *atara*, or collar, on his *tallit*. Otherwise, except for the respect and love that my father had for his father-in-law, there was no Hasidic element in my upbringing at all. My mother, the diplomat, became the referee in the Reguer family quarrels.

Uncle Chaim and Uncle Shimon, my father's only brothers, who both ended up living in the United States, had the traditional education provided by the yeshiva system of Lithuania. They both excelled, the former more than the latter. However, some time in their teens they were each exposed to the new writings coming in both from the West and from Russian writers, in particular Karl Marx. They were caught up in the new ideologies, and swallowed whole the viewpoint that religion was the opiate of the masses. Throwing off their "opium," they bore home the news of the wonders of Bolshevism, Menshevism, and Marxism. To underscore the contempt that Uncle Shimon in particular felt for Judaism, while still in Europe he had the temerity to smoke a cigarette in front of his own father on Shabbat. Their whole town heard about it, and my father never really spoke civilly to his brother again. I barely knew of his existence until my Aunt Golde, whom I was visiting at one point, mentioned his name.

Who is Uncle Shimon?, I asked my father. A brother of mine, was the terse reply. Why don't we have him up for Purim, like we have Uncle Chaim or Aunt Golde? He wouldn't come. Is he married? Does he have any children? He was married, his wife left him and went back to Russia with the son and left the daughter with him. Why? Not now. This was not a satisfying conversation, and it took some time to find out what I really wanted to know.

Uncle Shimon, it seems, was an active Bolshevik, but once the Revolution took place and antisemitism came to the fore, he had to get out of Russia quickly. He came with his wife and two children to New York City and set up a bee farm somewhere in New Jersey. But whenever he had any money, he would go to the city and spend it on concerts or operas, not caring anything about his family. His wife put up with it for a number of years, but finally packed her bags, took their son, and left her daughter Hilda behind, very unhappy to be abandoned, with Uncle Shimon.

When I was about nine, on an outing with my parents to Brighton Beach, we were walking along the boardwalk when I felt my father grow tense. He was looking intently at a scruffy older man who was looking just as intently at him from a few feet away. "Moshe Aron?," said the voice, one very much like our other family members and which emanated from a very suntanned face with the family's thick eyebrows. "Shimon?" was the response. This was how I met the Communist uncle who had been so nasty to my grandfather. He looked at me, and said, "Well, you have one at least that looks like the family. Have you poisoned her mind already?" My mother, ever the diplomat, stepped in to prevent a fight, asking about Hilda and Walt. Walt?, I wondered. Did I have another cousin? Was Hilda married to Walt? Walt, Uncle Shimon responded, was fine and was in second grade. How astonishing, and confusing! It seemed I had a cousin my age. And what kind of name was Walt? Seeing my confusion, my uncle said to my father, "I see that you don't even talk about us." To this, I responded: "Oh, yes, he does! I know that you smoked a cigarette in front of *Zayde* on Shabbos, and that you don't believe in God, and that you are a hobo." From the mouths of children. I did not see him again until my aunt's funeral, seven years later.

Despite the amount of time my father spent away from his family, I have not been able to find a record of written communication dating to earlier than 1936. Regards were probably sent orally, unless there was an emergency or a special event, such as his sister Feigl's wedding during World War I. Had there been any letters, I have no doubt that my father would have cherished them as he did his family photographs.

The earliest letters from my grandfather and my aunts date to 1936/1937, a year after my parents married. The conversation is one-sided, naturally, and I can only guess at what my father wrote in reply. The last letter in this small treasure trove is dated in 1941, at the same time as the Nazis broke their pact with Stalin and marched eastward, overrunning the rest of Eastern Europe and invading Russia.

My grandfather's letters are all formulaic in style, and address all of his American children. One can presume that they all shared the letters when they arrived. Between the lines, however, one can see slight differences in the way my grandfather addressed his children. For example, the only ones to receive the traditional religious formulations of "yichye" or "tichye"—a wish that they should be blessed to live long lives—are my parents and my cousin Charne, who was only a little girl at the time. When my father's ordination became official, he was addressed as "ha-rav" by my grandfather. I was interested to see that not a single letter has the Hebrew acronym B'H or B'EH (with God's help) up on the right-hand corner—that seems to have become *de reguer* only in contemporary times.

My grandfather's Yiddish is Torah Yiddish, and any traditionally educated Jew would recognize his references. My Aunt Esther's Yiddish, by contrast, is an educated Litvish type, and her letters are very newsy and very lively. There is only one letter from Peshke, the youngest sister, who does not seem as comfortable with the language as her much older sister was. The only letter from Moshe Reuven Gulewsky is in stilted Hebrew. His wife Feigl wrote nothing.

The translated letters are followed by my comments, which try to put them into context. There are inconsistencies in how they are written and punctuated, which have been retained: I wanted the letters to speak for themselves.

Simcha Zelig Reguer,
1930

Simcha Zelig Reguer,
1937

Simcha Zelig Reguer &
Moshe Aron Reguer, 1937

Simcha Zelig Reguer, 1937

Simcha Zelig Reguer, 1938

Sorke Reguer, Moshe Aron Reguer, Simcha Zelig Reguer, Moshe Reuven Gulewski,
Chaim Ber Gulewski, Feigl Gulewski, 1937

Simcha Zelig Reguer at funeral, 1938

Simcha Zelig Reguer,
Rabbi Velvel Soloveitchik,
1938

Center, Simcha Zelig Reguer,
Rabbi Velvel Soloveitchik,
1938

Anne Shabbason Reguer & Moshe Aron Reguer, 1936

The Letters

1. **Simcha Zelig (hereafter referred to as SZ) to Moshe Aron (hereafter referred to as MA)**

Date: probably 1936

> *My son ha-Rav Moshe Aron*, yikhye, *and daughter-in-law Chantche*, tikhye.
>
> *We received your letter. It gave me joy and I am happy that you bought a proper Vilna Shas. Hashem Yisborakh should help you, and your children too, learn from them and be good Jews. The Vilna Shas printed in New York has rejected many Talmudic novellae (hidushim) and not printed them even though they are vital.*
>
> *I wrote a receipt for Golde's photographs. Why my letter got lost, I do not know. Regards to Golde and her husband and child and to all [my] children and all our good friends.*
>
> *Simcha Zelig*
> *We are all well.*

In this letter, there are no paragraphs, and almost no periods. My grandfather jumps from one topic to the next. There is no date, and the envelope is lost.

Note that my grandfather addressed my father as *"ha-Rav"* with great pride. He knew of the existence of the New York edition of the Vilna Shas, as well as its omissions.

I know that my father bought the Shas himself after realizing that his father-in-law could not afford to buy him a set, which was the usual present from a father-in-law to a son-in-law upon a Litvak marriage. He was disappointed by these economic realities but realistic, and had deep respect and love for Reb Issachar Shabasson despite the enormous gap in education between them.

It is interesting to see that my grandfather signs his name, not "Father"; my father did the same in his letters to me.

2. SZ to all his children in New York
Date: June 2, 1937

My son Shlomo Chaim, and my son Shimon, and daughter-in-law Gitl, and their daughter Hilda, and their son Berl, and my daughter Golde, and her husband Moshe Ginsburg, and their lovely daughter Charne Rochel (tikhye), and my son ha-Rav Moshe Aron (yikhye), and his wife/partner (zug) Chantche (tikhye):

I have not written a letter in a long time.

M.A.: That which you write that "kol dikhfin yeitsei ve-yeikhol" is an act of burning (destruction) which is an act of destroying (shmita fruit). [Shmita fruits have to be destroyed or made ownerless. There is a period of time during which all shmita fruit has to be physically removed from the house. See Rambam, "Hilkhot Shmita" 1:7—Ed.] *But you may not take this ownerless fruit home. This is not "bi'ur" (destruction).*

You were in Eretz Israel—what kind of maror does one eat in Eretz Israel? I heard that "khrein" (horseradish) does not grow there. [Note that he presumed that "maror" was horseradish, like a good Litvak, when there is no mention of that root in the Mishna, and horseradish was considered more sharp than bitter—Ed.]

I suffer, but that is not news.

When it comes to practical things, you rely on the woman. [One can extrapolate from this statement that my father must have asked something about kashrut and cooking—Ed.]

May the Almighty help with all good things.

Tell Golde to write about her Charne Rochel. How is she? Does she speak some words yet?

We are well. Mother is as usual.

Zippora went off to America.

This summer we emptied the little room for Mother. [My grandmother's condition was gradually deteriorating, after her stroke ten years earlier. It was more practical for her to stay in the small room, and not in the bedroom—Ed.]

Chana Peshe [Feigl's daughter] came home for
Pesach.
   Simcha Zelig

My grandfather wrote on one quarter of a yellowed page; Esther filled up ¾ of the letter—her portion is summarized below. Note that my grandfather addresses only Charne, Moshe Aron, and Chantche with the "yikhye/tikhye" blessing, for he certainly knew how religious and observant his other children were, but had hopes for Charne.

This letter has no punctuation and no paragraphs, and the majority of it is written in response to my father's questions, which we can only guess at.

Note my grandfather's interest in the type of "maror" used in Israel, and his knowledge that horseradish does not grow there.

On a subtle note, the word used for my mother, "zug," has overtones of happiness, indicating my grandfather's confidence that my father had found a true match.

[The following is a shortened version of Esther's letter:]
We await your visit. [This statement is addressed to
my father.] Nothing is new here. Mother is very weak.
Father is as usual. Feigl has big tzoros from Chanale.
She is probably better off at home. She doesn't know
what to do. You understand that for a mother there is

nothing worse (than a sick child). They hired a tutor and a girl to go with her. Enough tzoros.

No news with me. The children should be well. They are sick every Monday and Tuesday because Peshke brings the colds home from school. The doctor told me to go to Krinitze (on the sea) for my health. What is doing with Golde? Chaim? Shimon? Golde doesn't write.

Peshke came for Pesach. She is well set up and has work [in Warsaw].

Be well and regards to your wife. I enclose a photo of my Rokhl dressed up like Shirley Temple for Purim.

There is no signature, and the letter is only addressed to my father.

Feigl and Moshe Reuven's older child, Chana, either had brain damage or was retarded, as was briefly touched upon above. They tried to send her to a facility, but it didn't work out at that time. Their second child, Chaim Ber, was healthy. The fact that there were no more children reflects on their bad marriage, and might also suggest that Feigl used birth control to make sure she would have no more children like Chana. She had done her duty by producing a son. Her marriage was a disaster.

3. SZ to MA and ASR

Date: 24 VIII 1937

Greetings for a very happy New Year [A long greeting in Hebrew is omitted here.] ... *To my son* ha-Rav ha-harif, moreinu ha-rav *Moshe Aron and to his partner (zug) my dear daughter-in-law Chantche (tikhye).*

Yesterday I sent the documents from the [Polish] Office of "Morals" (Religious Overseers) to Cherbourg to your address on the ship [taking you back after your visit]. If it misses you it will be returned to us. We will then send it to Brooklyn to your address.

The letter that came on Shabbes *from Canada I just opened now, and when I saw that it was written in Yiddish, I did not read it and I put it into an envelope and forwarded it to Brooklyn.*

I wish you and your wife Chantche a good year.

[Blessings in Hebrew follow.]

Simcha Zelig

Note the new greeting for my father, because he officially received his *smicha* from the Bet Din of Brest-Litovsk while he visited that summer. The copies of the *smicha* were sent to America (see the letter from Moshe Reuven). My father must have tried to obtain various documents from the Polish government office where rabbinical ordinations were registered while he was visiting, but it took too long and he had to return to America before completing the paperwork.

The return address on the envelope in which I found this letter is "Listowskiego 42, Ryjer, Brzesc n/B (net Bugem:Bug River). The letter is on one side of a piece of paper torn in half. In the same envelope, though they did not necessarily arrive together, is a note from Peshke—the only one—and a postcard from my grandfather to Chaim Ber in his yeshiva in Kletzk. How my father obtained these two letters is unknown, but they were in the collection. The date of Peshke's letter has to be at least 1938, as she got married in November 1937 and gave birth a year later.

Peshke to Simcha Zelig
[Undated, handwriting seems to show that she was not that comfortable writing in Yiddish—or perhaps she just had bad handwriting.]

Dear Father,

Yesterday I received a letter from you [asking] if you would be able to send some things—warm things for the "mother" (she had just given birth) and a warm hat and a warm costume (suit) with socks and shkarpen, all warm.

Yesterday I made a photograph and it will be ready in ten days.

I can't write any more because Mother hates me.

Regards to all.

Yours, Peshke

4. SZ to MA and ASR

Date: September 1, 1937

[Three lines of greetings for Rosh Hashana in Hebrew are omitted.]

Greetings for the New Year, may you be inscribed for life among the list of the holy ones. To my son the "sharp" rav, "moreinu ha-rav" Moshe Aron (nero ya'ir) and his partner, my daughter-in-law Chantche (tikhye), may the Almighty fulfill all of your wishes for good things.

I wrote to you but my letter never arrived. So I had some aggravation. You did not tell me that you requested the documents for the [Polish Government] Office of Morals be handed in by the community (kehilla). You should have done this as soon as you arrived. You should have written to the community through our relative Rabinowitz and through Avremel. On the Wednesday after you left, the community returned the documents to me. They said that they could not hand in the documents [as they are]. I had the attestation to your qualifications signed by Rabbi Klepfish and Rabbi Leib Eisen. I am a father and so could not sign it myself, and the Kehilla understood this. They stamped it and sent it on Monday to the "Cherbourg" to your address. But something went wrong and the packet came back. I will resend it to the proper address in Brooklyn. I have a document from the Rabbinate and can send that to you too. When it arrives, please let me know.

Chaya Feigl is still away with Esther and the children at the seaside.

We are well.

Mother is as always.

Simcha Zelig.

Note all of the titles given to my father now that he was given official rabbinic status by the Kehilla. This all has to do with the documents that were supposed to be signed by the Kehilla and then submitted to the Polish Office of Morals for registration.

Esther went every summer to the Baltic Sea where she rented rooms in a Polish house; this enabled Feigl to get away from all the tensions of home.

My grandfather's letter was written on two sides out of four included in the letter; Esther wrote a scribbled note on one side. She had just returned from vacation and had come by to greet her father. The letter was written using terrible paper and ink.

5. SZ to MA and ASR

Date: November 14, 1937

To my son Moshe Aron, yichye, *and my daughter-in-law Chantche*, tichye.

I have not written in a while and I haven't received a letter from you in a while. I ask you to write about everyone. I have one new thing to write. I wrote a Rosh Hashana *greeting to Rabbi Moshe Azaliion* [?] *as I write every year and I wrote to Rav Moshe's son a* Rosh Hashana *greeting and nothing came back to me as usually did each year. Perhaps I don't have their correct updated address. Perhaps they moved.*

Write what is happening with you. Maybe there is happy news. How is Charne Rochl? You gave regards to Rav Moshe Horodner [?] *or have you forgotten?*

Dr. Churgin, I am guessing is the Pohoster (Belorussia) Rov's son and a son-in-law of Rabbi Yoel Paltover [?], *of blessed memory, who was Rosh Yeshiva in Zvahil* [perhaps this is Zavhil—Ed.].

You also told me that you saw a number of my acquaintances. I told you that I want to know if they invited you to their cities.

I told you that the fish sterliab *in Russian and* shteher *or* shtirl *in German was allowed by the* Nodeh BeYehudah. *How does the world of America feel about this? Do they accept it as a kosher fish or not?* [**There**

197

Letter 5

is a difference of opinion over whether certain fish are kosher. There is more on this in the following letter—Ed.]

We are all well. Mother is as always. Peshke probably wrote to you that she got married.

Simcha Zelig

As usual, there are no paragraphs and almost no punctuation. My grandfather repeatedly refers to what was said earlier. The one legal issue discussed has to do with the fish, which is dealt with in another letter.

Note how the *yichus* issue plays out.

There is constantly the worry about letters arriving.

My grandfather waited until the final line of his note to mention the marriage of Peshke, which shocked everyone.

Also, there is the hint about "happy news" my father, who by now had been married over a year and a half, might wish to share.

Esther's letter is attached to my grandfather's:

Peshke suddenly got married in Warsaw without anyone knowing. This greatly saddened our father. Our brilliant sister? Everything is so crooked (twisted) with her. She is pretty, intelligent, etc. and married an old (in his forties) stupid tailor!! [She rips her sister apart and predicts that she will regret this marriage very much. She went to Warsaw and returned heartbroken at Peshke's decisions. Esther partly blamed herself—Ed.]

Dr. Pinchos Churgin (1894-1957), referred to above, was at the time of the writing of the letter dean of Yeshiva University's Teachers' Institute. He became my father's mentor, eventually hired him to teach in the Teachers' Institute, and urged him to work toward a doctorate. Without his encouragement, my father's career would probably not have moved in the direction that it did.

6. SZ to all the American children
Date: April 1938

To my son Shlomo Chaim, and my son Shimon, and my daughter-in-law Gitl, and their daughter Hilda, and their son Berl, and my daughter Golde and her husband Moshe Ginsburg and their daughter Charne Rochel, tikhye, *and my son Moshe Aron,* yikhye, *and my daughter-in-law Chantsche,* tikhye.

Today I received twenty-five dollars. I understand that there is also a receipt for the pictures of Charne Rochel. I received it and I think I wrote a receipt.

Write what is going on with you. Does Charne Rochel speak any more words yet? How are all of our acquaintances? Have you, Reb Moshe Aron, anything good to tell? I have pain. What is doing with Reb Shlomo (probably Heiman)?

I wish you a kosher and happy Pesach.

Simcha Zelig

Mother is as always. We are all well.

Moshe Aron: I received your letter after I wrote [the above]. I hoped that you would meet with [illegible names].

You made a mistake in writing that they wanted to take Rav Shlomo in Rav Shimon's place. Rav Shimon (presumably Shkop) should live a long time. That means his son-in-law's place, who died. **[These are references to yeshiva politics, and which positions have been opened due to the deaths of the holders—Ed.]**

I misplaced your letter but then found it. It is not the fish that the Nodeh BeYehuda zts'l allowed. The fish that you describe is described in Tiferet Yisrael sixty years ago. There was a dispute among the rabbis because one can see scales through a microscope. The Tiferet Yisrael says that they did not know French. In French it is the fish barduta, *which Rabbenu Tam allowed but other Tosfot forbade. And in* Avodah Zara, *page 40, Tosfot says that the fish has scales but it loses them when it is taken out of the water. From where Tosfot knows this we do not know. And in* Hulin *page 64, Tosfot says we don't know if it has scales that it loses when taken out of the water. But the Nodeh BeYehuda, zts'l, identifies the fish with what is called in* Russian sterliyad *and in German* shtirl, *a fish which has two rows of scales that you see without a microscope, but we cannot remove the scales. Yet the*

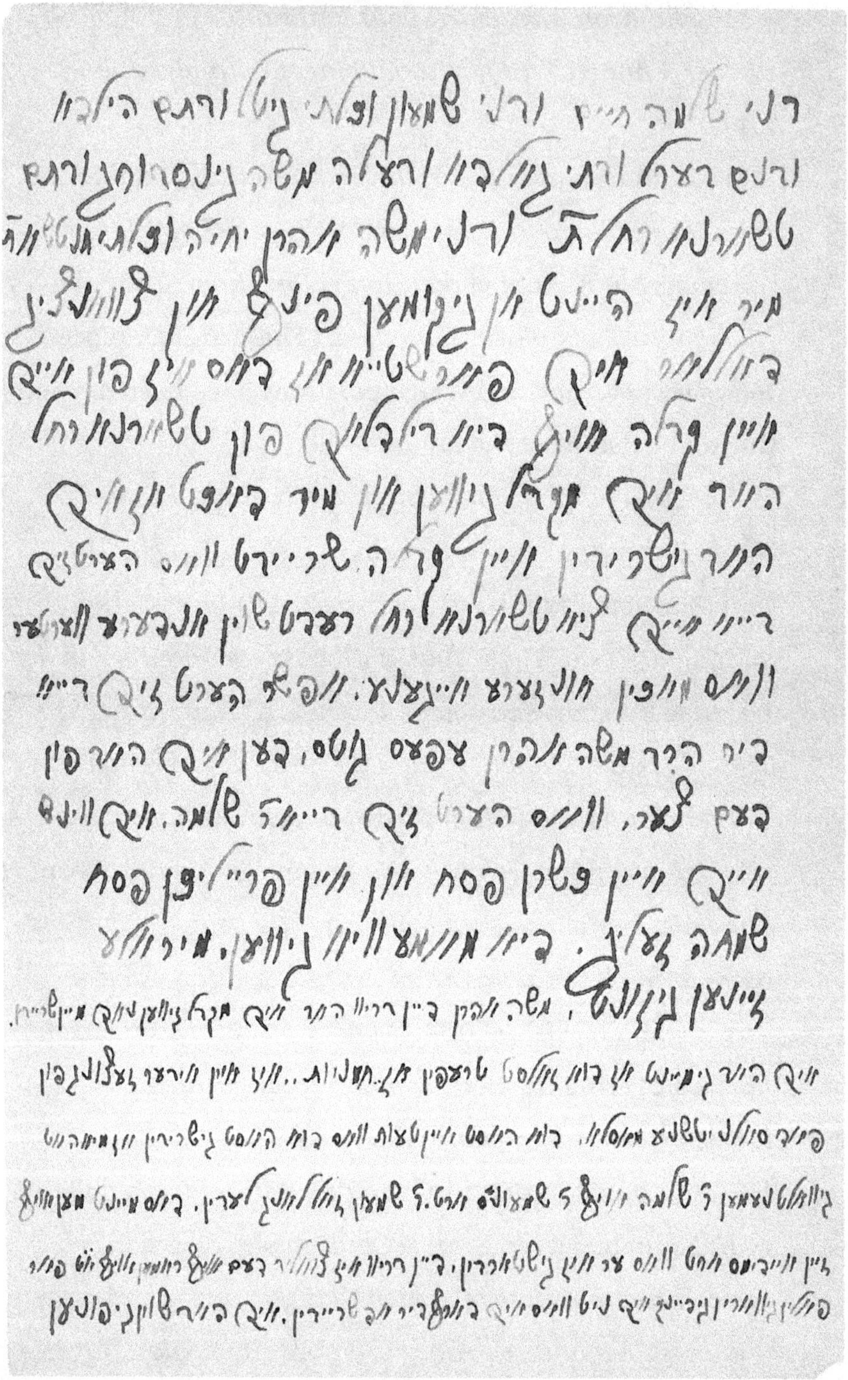

Letter 6

Nodeh BeYehuda, zts'l, soaked it in lye and the scales could be removed. [**The controversy over sturgeon and what makes a fish kosher is in Israel Meyer Levinger's** *Encyclopedia of Kosher Animals*—**Ed.***]

Have a kosher and happy Pesach, you and Chantche. I should live to see from you religious generations, great in Torah and Yir'at shamayim.

Simcha Zelig

Esther wrote on two sides of the page for her letter. She was preparing for Pesach. She had gone to Warsaw to see a doctor as she didn't feel well, and her daughters needed a healthy mother. Her only comment about the political situation is that "things are bad for all Jews, but it is our bad luck for it to be really bad."

She had visited Peshke in Warsaw, and reported that she was well set up"and bought a nice apartment with our money." Chana would be home for Pesach and Chaim Ber was already there. She was concerned about exchanging photographs.

7. SZ to all the children
Date: Before the summer of 1938

To my son Shlomo Chaim, my son Shimon, my daughter-in-law Gitl, their daughter Hilda, their son Berl, my daughter Golde (tichye), her husband Moshe

---

* (New York: Feldheim, 2011), 331-333.

*Ginsberg (yichye), their lovely daughter Charne Rochel
(tikhye), and my son the Rav moreinu ha-rav Moshe Aron
(yichye), and my daughter-in-law Chantche (tikhye):*

*I received two letters from Moshe Aron and one from
Golde. I am happy. I received regards from Moshe
Aron from Gotl "Baal Agala" (the wagon driver) and
Mekler, whose daughter wrote to him to give regards
from Moshe Aron, and regards from my brother, whose
grandson wrote to him with regards from Moshe Aron
and Chantche.*

*I put off responding because the papers scream war.
But it is better to write early. Benyomin Sikolovsky
writes from Russia that we should not write to him and
he will not write to us.*

We are all well.

Simcha Zelig

*Mother is as always. There is nothing to say. Moshe
Aron: What is in Hebrew* shemen khamaniyot?

*The photograph of Charne Rochl pleases
mother and all of us. She should be well. Chana
Peshe wrote a letter in Polish in her own handwriting.*

**This letter includes one side from my grandfather and three
sides from Esther. She basically writes about her girls, how they
are learning, and how they are reacting to their mother's constant**

health complaints. It is especially addressed to Golde to reprimand her for working too hard and hovering too much over Charne. If you overwork, she warns, your daughter will have no one. *"Father is the same, Mother is the same. And Feigl schleps along as always. It is killing us about Peshke, and don't say that she alone is responsible."* **Feigl** had been sending her money that she saved because, she insisted, Peshke had such a hard life that even after she was married she had to continue to work, never considering that this may have been preference rather than necessity. *"Maybe if you had been here, it would have been different."*

Here and elsewhere it is clear that Esther is a big complainer. The most my grandfather wrote along these lines was a brief sentence that he had "tzores."

There is only one brief reference to the political situation in Europe. The reference to Russia is connected to the realities of Soviet life. The normalcy of the letter is striking, as is my grandfather's obsession with addressing each individual member of the family and sending and receiving regards from anybody and everybody.

8. SZ to MA and ASR

Date: late August 1938

> *My son ha-Rav Moshe Aron (yikhye) and my daughter-in-law Chantshe (tikhye).*
>
> *It is very hard for me to write. Zalman already wrote to you that your mother, the* Tzidkanit, *is at her final*

rest as of Monday 25 Av, and on Tuesday she was buried. "May her soul be bound up in Eternal Life." It was a large funeral. The whole city was at the funeral. She is buried next to Rav Leibele Katzenelenboigen's Shtibele (ohel). I can only comfort you. "May the Almighty comfort you and us among other mourners of Israel and Jerusalem."

We take pleasure in that you visited her a year ago and she was happy about this visit. When the announcement came from you that Chantche is pregnant, I told her and she was very happy. May the Almighty help her to carry [to term] in health, and arrive at her "time" in good health, and have an easy birth, and she should be well and the child should be well.

You wrote that Chantche asked a she'ela—if she should fast on Tisha B'Av. Impossible, for the letter was written two days before Tisha B'Av. I perceive that she is asking if she must khoshesh zein—i.e., check for her period. In Yore De'ah 189, paragraph 34, it states that if she is carrying about three months, she does not have to khoshesh zein about her period. She must be careful not to carry a heavy load. May the Almighty help her be healthy [and carry to birth].

May you be inscribed for a good year, in the Book of the Righteous.

רʼ הרב משה וויתן יהיה ולבʼ חמשטשʼ ומזיה

וירʼ וייʼ נʼʼצר שʼʼאר לʼווʼ שוʼיירין. גʼאן השʼ בʼיʼ שʼוʼן גʼשʼיירין ואʼ

בʼין מאʼצʼ בʼיו לʼבʼפʼיʼא וויʼן וולʼאʼצʼ וויʼ זʼיʼהר רוו מʼשʼטʼיʼ פʼיʼאʼ

וʼון לʼוװʼמʼלʼגʼ טʼואʼ וʼין מר וייʼ גʼיʼ גʼשʼטʼואʼרʼין וʼון בʼיʼטʼוʼיʼ בʼוʼא

מאʼן וויʼהר מצרʼ גʼלʼאʼן. תהי נשʼמה. לʼרʼורʼ רʼבʼורʼ הʼתʼייʼק סʼאʼויʼ

גʼוʼלʼאʼן וʼין גʼרʼיסʼ לʼורʼ. גʼוʼלʼ שʼמʼוʼ וʼיʼ גʼיʼמʼוʼלʼאʼן וʼוʼ בʼצʼרʼ

לʼויה. ווʼיʼ הʼוʼ וויʼבʼרʼ מצרʼ גʼיʼלʼאʼן לʼצʼרʼין רʼ לʼיʼרʼאʼלʼʼ

שʼוʼיʼרʼאʼצʼ. וʼיʼ פʼאʼן בʼיʼ לʼחʼרʼ מʼאʼ צʼיʼין. הʼמʼלʼ יʼתʼ וʼלʼתʼ וʼוʼתʼ

רʼגʼ שʼוʼ וʼלʼיʼ לʼוʼן ורʼושʼלʼיʼמʼ. וʼיʼ טʼוʼ בʼאʼתʼבʼ וווʼ בʼאʼ הʼוʼסʼ

גʼיʼ גʼיʼאʼצʼבʼאʼן וʼשʼ זʼוʼהרʼ פʼיʼאʼ וʼזʼבʼרʼין וʼוʼן גʼיʼוʼ וʼשʼ גʼוʼלʼאʼן בʼיʼבʼין

וווʼסʼ בʼזʼ הʼוʼמʼסʼ גʼיʼ גʼיʼאʼצʼבʼאʼן וʼשʼ וʼיʼהרʼ. וʼאʼן אʼצʼ וʼיʼ וʼן גʼפʼואʼן

פʼין בʼיʼרʼבʼוʼ יʼצʼאʼ מʼן חʼמʼשʼטʼוʼ שʼרʼוʼגʼלʼ. הʼוʼרʼ מʼʼ בʼʼצʼרʼ גʼʼוʼ

גʼוʼלʼאʼן לʼוʼ בʼʼרʼיʼן. הʼʼ"תʼ וʼוʼ בʼʼצʼ פʼʼין וʼן גʼʼיʼ וʼוʼיʼ סʼטʼמʼעʼן גʼיʼוʼאʼאʼ

בʼיʼ. וʼלʼון הʼמʼרʼן לʼוʼ בʼצʼ בʼʼיʼ גʼיʼוʼאʼצʼרʼבʼʼ. וʼיʼן גʼיʼ וʼלʼ עʼיʼגʼ הʼמʼיʼן.

ווʼן גʼיʼ וʼלʼ גʼיʼ גʼיʼוʼלʼאʼ. וʼלʼ בʼוʼ פʼיʼבʼ וʼלʼ לʼיʼן גʼיʼוʼלʼ. בʼוʼ הʼוʼסʼ

גʼשʼוʼיʼרʼין חʼמʼשʼטʼוʼ בʼרʼאʼ טʼאʼ וʼאʼלʼאʼ. וʼיʼ פʼ בʼוʼאʼשʼוʼ וʼ גʼיʼוʼ פʼאʼנʼין

לʼוʼ וʼוʼן פʼוʼמʼטʼוʼ אʼצʼאʼ רʼורʼ. צʼאʼ טʼוʼ וʼיʼן וʼיʼ בʼוʼ רʼוʼ וʼיʼ גʼשʼוʼיʼרʼין

גʼוʼחʼמʼרʼין לʼוʼחʼוʼטʼוʼצʼ בʼוʼרʼ אʼצʼאʼ רʼוʼ. פʼלʼאʼ וʼיʼ וʼלʼוʼ בʼרʼוʼ לʼוʼ

בʼוʼרʼגʼ הʼוʼ 99 צʼיʼן וווʼ לʼוʼ וʼיʼ הʼבʼרʼ וʼאʼתʼ. שʼ.וʼבʼלʼ וʼוʼן יʼורʼ כʼצʼה סʼיʼן פʼʼ

I did not tell Golde because of the law against motzi
diba hu ksil*, *but the custom is for a son to be told
so as to say Kaddish. I will send her Rosh Hashana
greetings, but separately.*

*Moshe Reuven gave the eulogy for Mother in the
synagogue plaza, while we carried her.*

May we all have good news.

Simcha Zelig

Moshe Reuven wishes you a happy New Year.

This is a two-sided letter written only by him.

The *halakhic* issue discussed is whether a woman needs to
check for her period past the third month of pregnancy.

A custom is mentioned of informing only sons about the
death of a parent because of their obligation to say Kaddish.
Daughters would be told only after the shloshim, thirty days after
the death, so they would be exempt from shiva. Public eulogies,
however, were not only for men, but also for women.

A general concern is expressed that pregnant women should
not lift heavy loads.

Diplomatically, he waits until the very end to inform
my father that his despised brother-in-law gave the eulogy,
knowing how upset he would be. But from the photographs

---

* "He who spreads calumny is stupid," Proverbs 10:18. This refers to the laws of mourning, "Shulchan Arukh, Yoreh De'ah" 402:12.

taken at that time, it is clear that my grandfather was shattered by the death of his wife. The funeral was huge, and my uncle Zalman's letter adds more details, informing us that the event was covered in the newspapers and that photographers were there too.

9. SZ to MA and ASR

Date: [The wrong one is written on top by my father. It probably should be 15 X 1938, i.e. October 1938, judging by its internal content. Gabriel had not yet been born.]

To my son ha-rav Moshe Aron n'y *and my daughter-in-law Chantche* tihye.

I held on to your earlier letter. I gave it to the children. I will address what I remember.

The Yahrzeit must be made on the day of the death, not the day of the funeral, because the day of the death has a source in the gemara, "ke-yom she-met bo avi" *("Like the day in which my father died"). The Yahrzeit for your mother, aleha ha-shalom, is the 25th day of Av. This year it comes out on Wednesday, parshat Re'e. Kaddish is said for eleven months after the death, because* "mishpat resha'im be'gehinoam 12 chodesh" *("An evil person is judged to spend twelve months in hell"). Everyone must believe that his mother is not evil. It is enough to say Kaddish for eleven months. You should say Kaddish until the 24th of Tammuz and*

no longer. It is no nafka mina *that you started your
mourning later [than we did]. Mother needs no Kaddish
in the twelfth month, for she was not evil. If you say
Kaddish in the twelfth month it goes against "Honor
your mother." Only on the Yahrzeit must one say
Kaddish.*

*With regard to names: you should not argue with
your wife. One needs one name and it must be with the
agreement of the wife. The Rav* **[R. Haim?]***, of blessed
memory, used to say that when it comes to naming, the
law is to go according to the wife, for she gives birth, so
one gives the right to her.*

*When your letter arrived, I surmised that Golde does
not know [about the death of her mother], therefore if
you give Mother's name, she will certainly know. Golde
should not know. But then both of your letters arrived,
from you and from Golde, and I perceive that someone
told Golde, and she berates me.*

*The $25 arrived. Do not send me any more money.
Have in mind to marry off Hilda. She is already twenty
years old and she should marry. And if one marries, one
remains virtuous and not permissive. With God's help,*
bli neder, *I will also help when she marries; I have a
part of Gershkowitz's inheritance, which she left to me.*

*Chantche—I hope that with the Almighty's help you
will carry [your pregnancy] through with* mazal, *and*

that you will have an easy and timely birth and that
you will be healthy and the child will be healthy. The
Creator should have pity and all should be for the best.
May the Almighty help all of you with good things.

   Simcha Zelig

   If the name "Sara" that Chantche has is not used, it
does not count and the name may be given if she agrees.

   Write about Aharon Leib. Ask Rav Shlomo **[Heiman?]**
about Aharon Leib.

   It has become worse in Switzerland **[by this he meant**
Czechoslovakia]. *Hitler wants to take over Switzerland.*
Hitler holds that the half of Switzerland that borders
Germany is his, and the other half should also be his.

   You must push Rav Shlomo that he should act with
regard to this. If one must formalize it. You should
write to Aharon Leib. You have his address. Something
should happen through correspondence.

This letter included three sides of paper written by my grandfather; at the bottom is a note in a strange hand, probably that of Aharon Leib's father. It is possible that this was a reference to getting visas from America so they get out of Poland. This is one of the only places in my family's documents from this period with direct (although mistaken use of the name, perhaps on purpose) reference to Hitler and the political situation. The Anschluss had taken place in March 1938, when Hitler had merged Austria to

Gemany. In September he had annexed the Sudetenland, also called Western Czechoslovakia.

This letter is full of information on naming customs and their reasons. It reminds the recipient that daughters were to be protected from bad news and repeats over and over the laws and customs of Kaddish a child says for a parent.

My mother's middle name was Sara, but she dropped it officially when she married. She had never really used it. There is an Ashkenazi custom that a man should not marry a woman who bears the the same name as his mother. The same holds true for naming a daughter the same name as the mother.

10. SZ to MA and ASR
Date: after February 2, 1939

To my son ha-Rav Moshe Aron and my daughter-in-law Chantche:

I wish you mazal tov. I just received news from Shlomo Chaim that Chantche gave birth to a boy thirteen days into [the Jewish month of] Shvat. The brit *has already taken place, Wednesday,* parshat Yitro. *I give you mazal tov for the* brit *also. May the Almighty help you raise him to Torah,* hupa, *and good deeds. Amen. And you should have from him much satisfaction, he should be an honest Jew and fear God. The* pidyon ha-ben *comes out on Purim, Saturday night, if Chantche is not a daughter of a* kohen *or* levi. *May the*

*Almighty help that all should go well. Chantche should
be well and the child should be well and you should
have an easy upbringing. When you write a letter, you
should mention the name of the boy.*

Simcha Zelig

*Moshe Aron and Chantche: I ask you not to let the
baby sleep with his mother but in a separate little bed
or carriage. When a child was born to my father, z'l, he
learned all night and when the child awoke, my mother
of blessed memory, would have to get up from bed to
nurse the child and not take him into her bed.*

**My grandfather's message took up one side of one page; there are
two sides from Esther.**

*Your news was wonderful and cheered up Father, who
has been very depressed. I laughingly said that I have
a bride for the new boy. The family should get bigger.
Maybe Golde would have a boy too.* **[Golde only had
one child, as did Peshke. It could be that they were both
Rh-negative, as many Litvak women seem to be, and were
thus unable to have further children—Ed.]** *Feigl tells
me I should too. I'm happy with three girls. My oldest
just turned 9. Here there is nothing new. It should be
quiet in the world. Don't forget to send my mother's
photographs.*

Notice how automatic it was to sit down with the calendar and work out the dates for the circumcision and Pidyon ha-Ben—redemption of the first-born, traditionally done one month after birth. As is customary, my father did not mention the name of the boy because the circumcision had not yet taken place.

There are clues here about how depressed my grandfather was after the death of his wife. What no one knew at the time this letter was written was how sick my mother was—the doctor who attended the birth gave her childbed fever.

11. SZ to MA, ASR, and Gavriel
Date: after Purim 1939, before Pesach

> *To my son ha-Rav Moshe Aron* yikhye *and my daughter-in-law Chantche* tikhye *and their son Gavriel* yikhye
>
> *I wish you mazal tov for the* bris *of your son and for the name Gavriel which he was given. May the Almighty help that the mother Chantche should be well and that the little boy Gavriel should be well and have a long life, and should be a great scholar and a religious Jew. Furthermore, I give you mazal tov for the* pidyon ha-ben. *May the Almighty help that you should have much joy from him and an easy upbringing. He should be successful and healthy, he should grow to be a big mensch, and learn and be a religious and successful person.*
>
> *On Shabbat the eve of Purim, Chaya Feigl made, in honor of the* pidyon ha-ben, *a feast in the old-age home*

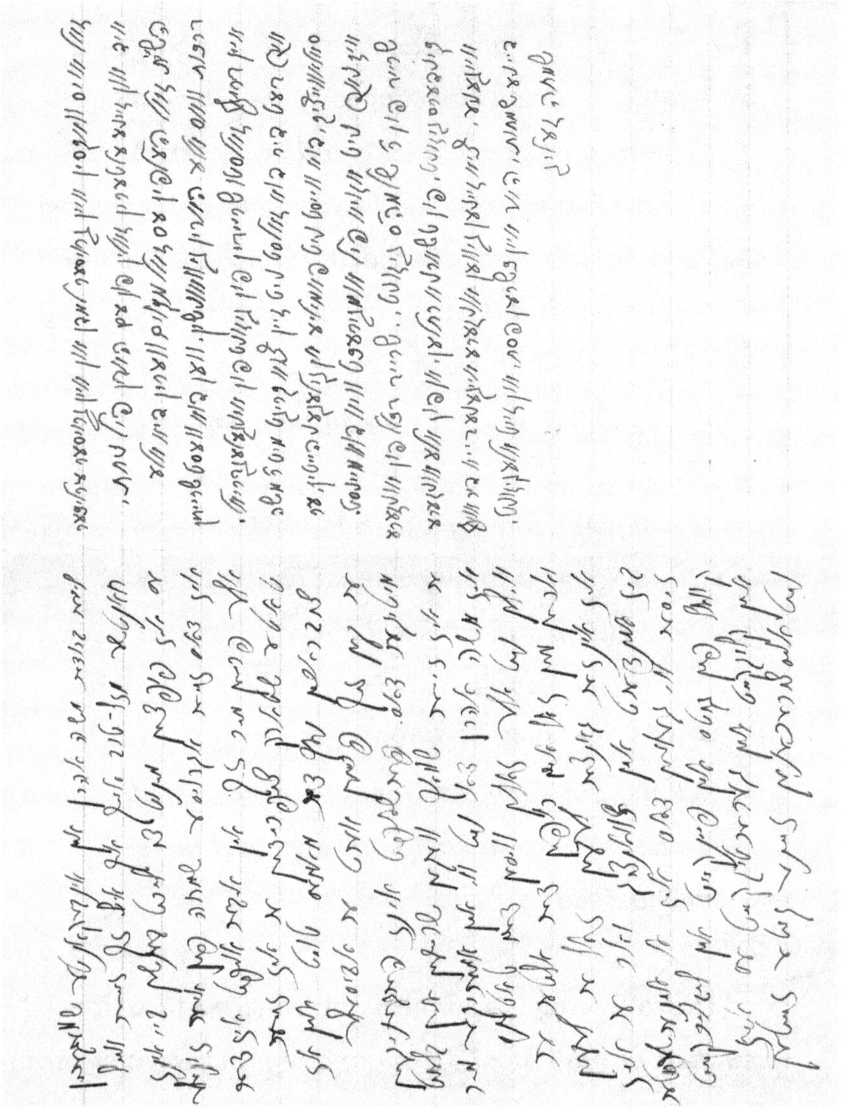

Letter 11

for the seventy-one old men and women. She carried over seventy-five hamantaschen and four bottles of drink and one small barrel of compote. The old men and women wished Chantche and baby Gavriel all the blessings. Chantche should be well and baby Gavriel should grow into a great scholar, an honest Jew, and his parents should have much nakhes from him. May the Almighty help this come true—all these blessings. When you will write, write about baby Gavriel's health.

I beg of you not to fight with Rabbi Moshe Soloveitchik. You do not know a family without opportunities (geleigenheiten), and he is not as wrong as you think.

Write about Rav Shlomo (Heiman)'s health. Write in general about our children's health, of Charne Rochel and of all our acquaintances. Were they at your celebrations? Have a kosher Pesach and be well.

Simcha Zelig

[The following is a summary of Esther's added note.] *To my dear brother Moshe Aron and my unknown sister-in-law Chantche—mazal tov. It is fifteen minutes to candle-lighting. It's a huge joy for us here about your baby boy. Father is enormously happy. He was shattered when Mother died. We don't want anyone to know this or "they" will call him* Der Alter. **[She goes on to say that she**

loves her father and thinks absolutely the world of him.
If he would die, she would want to also. She has major
problems, but loves her children. She does not understand
why Golde didn't go to the circumcision—couldn't she
have taken her child with her?]

It is interesting to note how the family celebrated—by
sharing with the poor and old. We are told the number of residents
of the old-age home. The fact that Brisk had such a home indicates
that there were many who did not live with their extended families
as they aged. The home was supported by the community.

There is another reference to the fighting with Rabbi Moshe
Soloveitchik. My grandfather asks as always about Rav Shlomo
Heiman, but he never asks about his wife, who was Sorke's niece.
Perhaps there was a cultural reason not to ask about a wife.

Finally, it seems that it was a bad thing to be called *Der Alter*.
Esther did not want my father to tell anyone in America how old
Simcha Zelig was.

12. SZ to MA and ASR

Date: after Purim, before Pesach 1939

> *To my son, Moreinu ha-Rav Moshe Aron,* nero ya'ir *and
> my daughter-in-law Chantche,* tikhye, *and their son
> Gavriel* yikhye.
>
> *I have received your letter. We had much pleasure
> from it. May the Almighty help you, that you should raise*

him to Torah, hupa, *and good deeds. He should be an
honest Jew, a Torah scholar, and a doer of good
deeds. You should have* nakhas *and have an easy
upbringing.*

*The Torah that you wrote is very good. Please
thank Rabbi Pinchas Churgin for me—he must be the
Azarnitzer Rav's son-in-law's brother. You did not write
that Rav Moshe [which one?] who learned in Volozhin
Yeshiva was at your celebrations. I already wrote
a mazal tov for the circumcision.*

*I have your letter. I beg you not to fight with Rav
Moshe Soloveitchik; he is not our enemy. If one looks
[at the world] with a bad eye, one judges others* le-khaf
khova *(negatively). One can always twist someone into
an enemy. But if one looks (at the world) with a good
eye, and judges* le-khaf zkhut *(positively), he becomes
a good friend. "Cover all sins with love."*

*May the Almighty help the baby, Gavriel, be healthy,
a Torah scholar, and fear God. You should have much
nakhas from him.*

*Have a kosher and happy Pesach. We are well.
Chaim Ber came for Pesach from Kletzker Yeshiva. He
learns quite well.*

Simcha Zelig

*Give regards to all the children, and to Charne
Rochel. It is hard for me to write to each separately.*

They should all have a happy kosher Pesach
   Simcha Zelig
   I thank all who were at the circumcision and pidyon-ha-ben.

This letter contains a message only from my grandfather, written on both sides of one page.

The fight with Rabbi Moshe Soloveitchik that is repeatedly referenced was possibly caused by Rav Moshe walking out of Takhkemoni of Warsaw, leaving my father without *smikha* (ordination). Litvaks have very long memories for insults and bad experiences. This unhappy history certainly did not affect my father's relationship with Rav Moshe's son, Rav Dr. Joseph B. Soloveitchik.

Note the *yikhus* reference to Dr. Churgin—that was how one was identified in this society.

Chaim Ber came home every Pesach.

13. SZ to MA, ASR, and Gavriel
Date: May 15, 1939

To my son ha-Rav Moshe Aron nero yair *and my daughter-in-law* tikhye *and their son my grandson Gavriel* nero yair.

The Tanakh translated by Yehoash arrived.

Write how Gavriel is. What do you hear from Golde?

How is Charne Rochel? And how are all our friends?

15-V-39

We are all well, thank God. Chaim Ber is learning in
Kletzker Yeshiva.

May the Almighty give us a happy Shavuot.

Simcha Zelig

You should say Kaddish *until Wednesday,* Mincha *of*
24 of Tammuz. The Yahrzeit *is the 25ᵗʰ of Av.*

This letter contains only a half-page from my grandfather, basically just acknowledging the receipt of the book, and two sides of a page written by Esther. Yehoash [Solomon Blumgarten], 1870-1927, was born in Jewish Lithuania and emigrated to the United States in 1890. Settling in New York, he wrote all kinds of intellectual works in Yiddish. His translation of the Tanakh is considered a monument to the language. It was published in New York and must have cost my father quite a bit, both to buy it and ship it.

Esther's portion of the letter is more expressive. After referring to the general political situation—*"You know the political situation. So does everyone. May God help us remain alive."*—she spends much of the rest of her letter describing her daughters. She discussed again the exchange of photos, with one side comment that their father was weak. Her husband Zalman was about to leave for the United States to attend the World's Fair, if all of his documents were put in order in time.

14. SZ to MA and ASR

Date: Probably June or July 1939

(wrong date penciled in on top)

> *To my son ha-Rav Moshe Aron* n'y *and my daughter-in-law M. Chantche* tihye *and their dear son Gavriel* yihye

> *We are wondering why you write nothing to us about Gavriel, may he be well.*

> *We stopped saying Kaddish. The last time it was said was Wednesday at* mincha *of* Parshat Matot-Masei. *The Yahrzeit is Thursday the 25 of* Menahem Av.

> *Zalman is leaving for America tomorrow. We are sending with him an arba* kanfot *for Gavriel.* **[This is a traditional garment now usually referred to as tzitzit. Included are instructions for putting it in water and bleach—Ed.]**

> *Write to us everything about everyone.*

> *I want to say again that Hilda should get married. In America there is no need for a dowry, therefore she can get married.*

> *Be well.*

> *Simcha Zelig*

This letter mentions that my grandfather said Kaddish for eleven months, even though it is not mandatory for a bereaved husband to do so. The dates are included as a gentle reminder for my father.

Simcha Zelig and the Brisk branch of the family probably thought that there were no good *tzitziot* in America, so they sent one from Brisk. My mother, however, knew how to make them herself.

Zalman Chary came to the United States for the World's Fair that was held in 1939 in New York City. The war broke out while he was in the United States, and he never made it back to Poland. He was the only member of the family to survive the war.

15. The last letter, which is really everyone scribbling a quick message to be taken by Rabbi Yaakov Muler, the Yashuner Rav, to mail in Russia so it could travel via Asia to the United States, as the war broke out in September of 1939.
Date of arrival: December 1939

[There is only one line from my grandfather:] *We are all well. Peshke and her husband Aharon are well and in Brisk.*

[Esther wrote the majority of the letter:] *To Chaim, Shimon, Golde, Moshe Aron, and Zalman: We are all alive, thank God. Writing about all that we lived through is impossible. It would take the long summer days and the long winter nights to tell all the miracles that happened to us. Your Father was in the greatest danger. It was a miracle that he survived. The*

Rabbi M. A. Reguer
1604 – 49 th Street
Brooklyn, N.Y.
U.S.A.

Schary Cohen
68 nassau street
new-york

arrived
7 Dec. 1939

Letter 15

[Russians] cut off his long beautiful beard. Zalman's business was sold. Most important, our daughters and I are still alive and so is everyone else. It's hard, but we are all alive. I only hope that our daughters get through this. May God help us survive. Love from the children, our wild wonderful girls.

[Moshe Reuven to Zalman:] *Esther sold the business and has a document attesting to it.*

On September 1, 1939, one week after the signing of the Molotov-Ribbentrop Pact, Poland was invaded by Germany. On September 17, the USSR invaded from the east. On October 6, 1939, Germany and the Soviet Union divided and annexed all of Poland. The Soviet Union incorporated its Polish provinces into the Belarus and Ukrainian republics and began to "Sovietize" the areas. But before that, on September 22, the Soviets and the Nazis met in Brest-Litovsk for a joint victory parade.

It is probably during this early occupation of Brest-Litovsk that my grandfather had the demeaning experience described. The Soviets probably decided that they could humiliate all of the Jews by humiliating their leading rabbi. My grandfather was already in his seventies, with a long, white, flowing beard. The Russians held him and cut it off. Menachem Begin witnessed this, as he attested when he met my father many years later in Jerusalem. Begin came from Brest-Litovsk, and his father was killed there in 1941.

On June 22, 1941, Hitler broke the pact with the Soviets and attacked eastward, in the beginning of Operation Barbarossa. After the initial executions of thousands of Jews in Brest-Litovsk, the Nazis built a ghetto there, which was completed on December 16. There were waves of excecutions over the next few months, and the beginning of the end of the ghetto was in October 1942. My grandfather and all of the males of the community were shot in the execution pits on October 14/15, 1942, 3/4 Mar Heshvan. The women were executed the following day. People who survived, mainly by pretending to fall dead, later sent my father attestations as to what they had witnessed.

The letters translated above and commented on were all written by my grandfather and my aunt, writing on the same stationery. The following letters were written by various other members of the family, such as my uncles by marriage, or, separately, by my aunt. I chose not to put them into chronological order, as the main focus of the book is on my grandfather. These can be viewed as sidebars rather than as part of the main text.

16. Moshe Reuven Gulewsky to MA
Date: late August 1937, after MA left Europe

> *To my brother-in-law the scholar (*ish ha-eshkolot*)*
> *Moshe Aron Reguer n'y.*
> *It took great effort on my part to obtain the*
> *documents for you because our brother-in-law Zalman*

traveled immediately to swim and bathe in the Baltic Sea. And even if he would have been in the city he would not have been able to do anything, because all of the institutions refused to fufill the request because it does not interest them. It seemed that I labored in vain, but we are satisfied now that we did not labor in vain.

Your father knows nothing of what happened to you "on the road," and to mislead him I wrote that you need the document in order to become a citizen.

If possible, please write the details of your trip but to Zalman's address.

Here there is nothing new. This week Esther and her daughters returned from Damatzuba (the Baltic coast), as well as Feigl, who spent a week and a half there].

Of course write details of your visit with Chana Peshe, even though the doctor (Korchak) was not there. Anyway you had a chance to speak to the teachers about her and you spent a few hours talking to her. How does she appear to you? Her development, her thinking, her intelligence?

We have no news. Send regards to "ours" [i.e., **their family and friends**] and a Happy New Year.

I am sending the documents to you. I made two copies, one I sent to the ship and the second I kept, for I predicted that you might travel on another ship *and so the letter would not reach you and would get lost even though we sent it "Special Delivery." I will now send the second copy to you. In my opinion it is unnecessary, but your sisters Feigl and Esther insist on sending it and I am following their wishes.*

I wish you a happy New Year—may God fulfil your wishes.

Moshe Reuven

They are asking about your wife's health.

I myself wrote the Yiddish translation and sent it to be translated into Polish and I packed the documents this way; otherwise they could not have been mailed.

Moshe Reuven wrote this letter in Hebrew, probably to show my father that he was not the only one who knew the language well. The Hebrew is clumsy and old-fashioned.

The tone of the letter is conceited, and the bad relationship between the two can be seen easily when one reads between the lines. He addresses my father as a scholar, using a very old term, and not "rabbi," even though my father had *smicha* by this point. More to the point, he refers to what happened "on the road," or "along the way," as a snide aside to the years my father spent in Palestine studying secular subjects at Hebrew University rather than in a yeshiva.

He wants full credit for getting my father's documents and for sending them to America. He also wants to know about my father's visit to his brain-damaged niece, Moshe Reuven's daughter, in Korchak's institution in Warsaw. My father told me about the visit, how Chana recognized him, how he tried to help by offering to bring her to America, and how he was told that nothing could help her. She died at the hands of the Nazis with all of the other children in the institution and with Dr. Korchak, who could have saved himself, but chose not to abandon "his children."

17. Zalman Chary to MA
Date: August 24, 1938

Dear Moshe Aron:

You must be wondering why I am suddenly writing to you. Your father asked me to inform you that your mother died on Monday at 2 p.m., and August 23 was her funeral. I have never in my life seen such a fine funeral for a woman. The synagogue plaza (shulhof) and all of the streets around it were packed with people. Our brother-in-law Moshe Reuven gave the eulogy on all of her good qualities and the good things that she did during her life. Moshe Reuven spoke with emotion for over an hour. Over a thousand mourners came from all walks of life, women and men, all crying like children the entire way to the cemetery. The greatest tzaddik does not get as much respect as your mother did.

When she died, none of her children was with her. My Esther just came in from Krinitze [where she spent her summer vacation]. Your Peshke was not told—your father said not to because she is pregnant. Only Feigl was there, and she cried and begged forgiveness a thousand times.

Reb Simcha Zelig said Kaddish alone in his tear-laden voice, and the whole crowd cried. Even the gravestones were crying. Everyone will remember this forever. There were even photographers on the way, photographing, and I will send you copies. Life is a dream. Everything is hevel-havalim. There is nothing one can say when you lose a mother, but you must have strength, for you do not live only for yourself. You have a lovely wife at your side.

Moshe Aron—your father asked me to have you tell Chaim and Shimon that they should say Kaddish. It will be hard to do, Moshe Aron, but you must obey your father. But do not tell Golde—he says strongly NO on this matter, because she will have great anguish.

We should only hear good news. Special regards to your wife Chantshe. Next year we will see you in America. I plan to come for the World's Fair.

Your brother-in-law,

Zalman

Zalman Chary writes what my grandfather told him to, plus what he wants to write too. My grandfather knew that his

two older sons would not want to say Kaddish for their mother, but asked my father to inform them anyway. He also made the decision to protect two of his daughters—pregnant Peshke and sensitive Golde.

Zalman also knew that my father would be very upset to learn that Moshe Reuven gave the *hesped* when the relationship between them was so bad. Seeing such a big crowd probably goaded Moshe Reuven into giving a one-hour speech, far longer than a *hesped* for a woman usually went. The photographers' presence probably influenced him as well. They were there because my grandmother was the wife of the Brisker Dayan, and they must have been alerted to the fact that there would be a huge funeral. There are surviving photographs from this event still in the family.

Zalman wrote beautifully, and was well educated. His relationship with his in-laws was a good one, and he had great respect for his father-in-law.

According to this letter, it seemed that he was planning to come to America in 1939 with his wife. That did not happen. He came alone, any it was while he was in the United States that Hitler invaded Poland.

18. Esther to MA
Date: September 29, 1938

Dear Moshe Aron:

[A long list of complaints has been omitted here.]

Mother is three months in the earth. We are so sad and

if we had not seen it, we would still not believe it. She had thirteen children, and no one was at her deathbed. Feigl had just gone to her Chana, leaving Mother alone, and when she returned, Mother was gone, and she found her body on the ground.

The majority of the suffering is Father's.

All of Europe is fearful of war.

[Further complaints have been omitted, among them the fact that Golde had not written.] *Moshe Aron—tell Chaim and Shimon to say Kaddish for Mother. She had her stroke in part because of the aggravation they caused her by becoming men who do not go in God's way. (You have the photograph of Mother in the wig—make a copy and send it. Regards to Golde and tell her to write. We should all have good news. A good year from Zalman too—he was in Belgium. Regards to your Chantche.)*

19. Esther to MA
Date: November 17, 1938

My dear brother Moshe Aron:

[...] What is happening to us Jews is in de bletter— *everyone is depressed.*

[This portion of the letter can be summarized by the following: There was no news at home, Simcha Zelig was weak, and they had just fired the maid.]

I went to the doctor in Warsaw—he said that I was
just overtired and he told me how to live properly.
And so goes the money. I went to Peshke... You heard
that she had a baby boy. She doesn't know yet about
Mother. I don't know how Golde found out. Mother was
77. For us she was not old. It is three months since she
died. Father does not speak much, but you understand
his pain—what good is speaking?

[This portion of the letter can be summarized as asking
for news of the brothers who did not respond to letters and
sharing details about her three daughters.]

They are remodeling Father's house, bringing water
in (for an indoor toilet). It will cost thousands of zlotys,
but the price was brought down to 500 zlotys because
it is for him.

Sorke was born in 1861, Simcha Zelig in 1863.

This letter refers to the indoor toilet built by the community
for Simcha Zelig; it was completed just as the Nazis invaded
Brest-Litovsk, and he never got to use this luxury: the house was
confiscated by the invaders.

Esther's visit to a medical specialist suggests that she
probably had high blood pressure or was depressed.

20. Esther to Moshe Aron

Date: January 18, 1939

[The opening of the letter indicates that they were awaiting the good news of Gabriel's birth, and hoping all was normal and went well.]

No news here. You read the news in the papers. We are helpless. We have no control.

Father is busy all day. Feigl is busy with the house— she invites no one. Chana helps when she is told to. Chana is well but she always fights with people. She is quiet in the house and helps and learns. Chaim Ber learns in Kletzk—he is gowing to be a big boy. No news with me. The girls are wonderful. I sent photographs to you to make copies.

21. Esther to MA

Date: April 2, 1939

What is doing with your new son? Maybe he can help you write. Nothing special here. You know well what is doing here. We should all live through it.

With Father—we are preparing for the holiday. We are baking matzos. Chaimke (Chaim Ber) is here. **[More family news is shared here.]** *Regards from Zalman. We should all see each other again.*

Moshe Aron, Father just got your letter and he is so happy. It is sweet news in his bitter times.

22. Esther to Chaim

Date: July 22, 1940

[This is a very long letter with no new information. While it was not addressed to my father, he kept this letter, probably because they all shared letters when they got them.]

23. Esther to Zalman

No date—probably the summer of 1939.

[The context of this letter was that Zalman was away on business, and Esther was stuck in a small rented room in a town near the sea with the girls. The contents of the letter were all patter and gossip. The eldest daughter was taking care of Simcha Zelig—she was his "new wife," they joked. Peshke and her husband moved to Bialystok where they worked. She was happy with the child. Esther really felt sick.]

24. Zalman to MA from New York [The American Diamond Company]

Date: August 13, 1940.

I tried to telephone but there was no answer. Did you find Chantche's traveling documents? I am sending you Chaim's (Chaim Ber) letter from the yeshiva and Esther's last one too.

Golde sent Esther a long, sad letter.

They all wish you a good year.
It is very important for Esther to get your letters.
Keep in touch.

Those are the twenty-four letters that I found in my father's "treasure trove."

Neither Simcha Zelig, nor anyone else, put BH or BSD on the top of any letter. He usually did not even put a date.

My father must have opened his letters numerous times over the years, and he was not careful about replacing them in the correct envelopes. That is probably how the dates that he penciled in got mixed up.

All of the correspondents knew what was going on in Germany, yet they rarely referred to the situation. When they did, it was in a kind of code. Did they fear being spied on, or was this just Jewish paranoia?

The upshot of the letters is normalcy. They were concerned with family issues, with community news, and with keeping in touch with those who had left Brisk.

My grandfather was the sort of person who reminded others of their obligations. My father continued this path, constantly reminding the children of important dates.

The house in Brisk was where all the children gathered. Esther brought her girls to visit my grandfather, especially after Feigl's two children left—Chana to Korczak's insitution in

Warsaw, and Chaim Ber to the Kletzker Yeshiva. Esther was often alone with the girls because Zalman's business took him all over Europe and even to America in 1939. She lived in the rich part of the city, and constantly came back to her old home.

The relationships among the siblings in New York was strained. My grandfather knew perfectly well that his sons Chaim and Shimon were not religious. He relied on my father to continue the family line. Note that he placed more importance on this than on his daughters' children, and commented that Esther "only" had girls, and Feigl's name was no longer Reguer.

Pages from the notebooks containing *My Memoirs* manuscript.

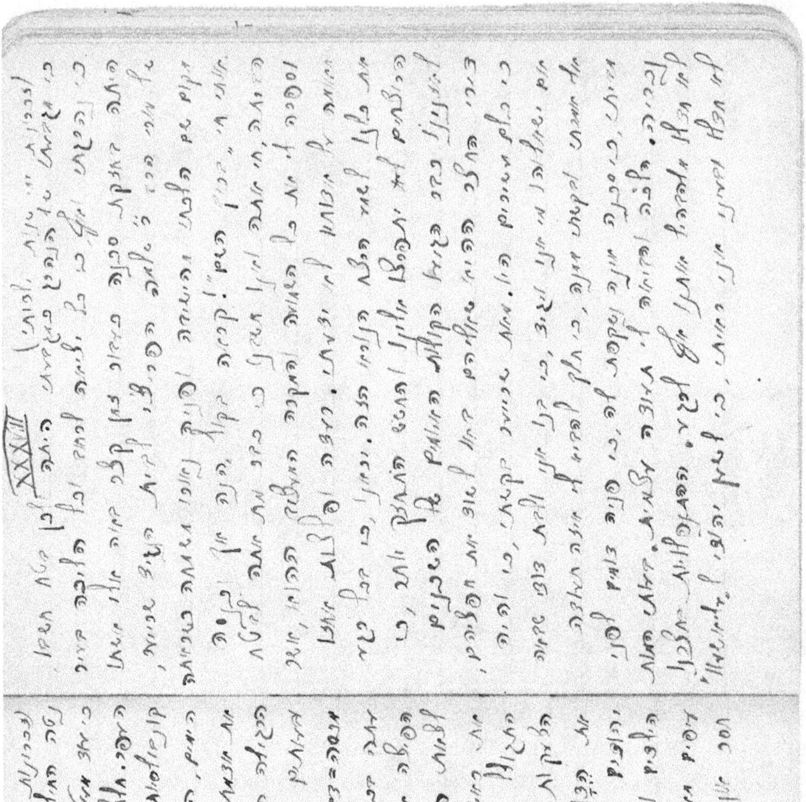

My father spent the war years worried about his European family. He tried to join the United States armed forces as a chaplain three times. At the start of the war, he was rejected because they were not taking married men. In the middle of the war, after Pearl Harbor and America joining on the Allied side, they would not take him because he had a child. By 1945, when he tried a third time, the war was over.

He had tried to get a visa to America for his father. He made every contact he could, asking everyone he could think of to help, including the heads of Yeshiva University. The visa was at last granted, but my grandfather refused to leave his community in Brest-Litovsk, claiming that it needed him. No one could have predicted that Hitler's war was against the Jews.

When personal news trickled in, and survivors of the Holocaust testified and sent letters to my father, he was horrified but realistic. He wrote down the dates of the killing fields, marking the third and fourth of Mar Cheshvan on his personal calendar.

Later on, he heard details from survivors such as Rav Meshullam Dovid Soloveitchik, who survived the war with his father Rav Velvel Soloveitchik. The details have been collected by Rav Shimon Yosef Meller. The Nazi invasion of the Soviet Union on June 15, 1941, led directly to Brest-Litovsk. The Nazis came to the house shared by the Soloveitchiks and my grandfather, and "ran up the stairs…. Moments later, they were seen leaving the building with the elderly Rav Simcha Zelig in tow. We saw him in the evening from a distance, bent over as if he were carrying a heavy weight. Rav Simcha Zelig moved heavily, broken and shattered, barely managing to drag his legs. His long beard had been hacked off, and his cheeks were bruised and bloodied…."

He had been taken to a military base, where the soldiers had interrogated him for hours. At the end of the exhausting questioning, a German officer approached him with a pair of sharp scissors and began cutting his beard with the coarse blades, which also wounded his face. But that wasn't enough for the German captors. After butchering his face, they threw him down a flight of stairs onto the street, calling after him that he should bring them five rubles the naxt day as payment for the "haircut" he had received.[*]

Months later, as the High Holidays neared, the Nazis forbade gathering in synagogues. Jews gathered clandestinely instead, in the ghetto where they had been confined. What little food there was, they shared. My grandfather continued to give his *shiurim*. On Yom Kippur 1942, the Nazis assembled the remaining Jews in the main synagogue, withheld their food, and cut off the beards and *payot* of the men. My grandfather consoled the others that these things were not that important to the Almighty, who considered every Jew important.

When the Nazis then demanded that a certain number of people should be handed over for excution, the Judenrat wanted to hand over Jews who had been forced into the ghetto from towns like Kovel and Chelm. My grandfather ruled that it was forbidden to differentiate between locals and newcomers, but the Judenrat did as they wanted.

Moshe Zeidman, one of the few survivors, has stated that my grandfather did not wear a *kittel* on Yom Kippur, explaining that the gemara states that people who die *"al kidush ha-Shem"* do not required shrouds, but are buried in their clothing in order to make a "storm" in Heaven.

Shortly thereafter, 4,000 Jews were marched to the killing pits which they had been forced to dig themselves, and were shot to death.

By this time, my father was in his forties. He devoted the second half of his life to his family and his students, collecting as many fragments of my grandfather's life as he could. Unwittingly, he passed down to us, his children, his father's family customs, which he had absorbed as a child. Often these customs were accompanied by the remark, "At home, my father did this."

On Shabbat, my father never sprinkled salt on his challa nor dipped his challa in salt after making the blessing, as was customary for many Jews. He always said that the salt was already baked into the challa.

---

[*] See Eliyahu Ackerman, "Posek for a World at War" in *Mishpacha* (May 23, 2012): 58-66.

Friday night *Kiddush* was said standing. Unless there were guests, he shared the wine with my mother. Each child had his/her own small silver *Kiddush* cup, and we went around the table according to age, reciting our own *Kiddush*. If a guest was present and shocked that a daughter made *Kiddush*, he told them that this was *chinukh*, education. It was not until I started going to other people's houses that I realized how special my father was in his attitude to women and Judaism. Did the girls do this in Brisk? I doubt it, but certainly the boys did. One thing that the girls did do around the Shabbat table in Brisk was join in the singing of *zemirot*. My grandfather had no voice for music, but he encouraged all of his children to sing.

By watching my father pray at home, I learned how he put on his *tallit* and *tefillin*. The largest *tallit* was held up above his head, reaching down his back, his hands held the edges up, and when he closed his fists together forming a tent, he said the blessing. As for the *tefillin*, the wrapping of the arm-strap was done toward the body (as opposed to away), and he used to make fun of the fact that I was ambidextrous, as it would have posed a good *halakhic* question had I been a boy—*tefillin* is customarily worn around the non-dominant arm. I mastered the intricacies of the wrapping of the strap around my left hand when I had to teach a basic Judaic Studies course at Brooklyn College.

We did not use *mayim aharonim* at the end of the meal, before the *birkat ha-mazon*, because my father said that we no longer had "salt of Sodom" to wash off.

Havdala was never said on milk, soda, or fruit juice; only grape juice, wine, or whiskey was used.

There are no special Rosh Hashana customs in our family, other than not having honey or sugar added to the baking of the challa, out of concern that sweetened bread would not take the blessing of "*ha-motzi*" but rather "*mezonot*." My father adapted to the unfamiliar fruits available in America, and liked to experiment. I learned what questions to ask the vendors in Chinatown as to whether the item I was considering grew on a tree or not, and learned the *halakhic* definition of a tree.

My father did not say *Tashlikh*, joking that Litvaks keep their sins from year to year.

I learned how to read ingredients. American Jews are lazy and rely on the kashrut supervision, said my father. Everyone should learn what lactic acid is, what ingredients (like gelatin) are not kosher, what is a meat product, and what is a milk product. He would bless the American legal system that demanded all ingredients be listed. And if there was just a drop of something, that was smaller in measurement than the American law demanded? *"Batul be-shishim"* was the response—it was less than a sixtieth of the volume, and so it didn't count. And then he would tell me not to be a *haredi*, a fanatic. "Judaism is not black and white, but shades of gray." These words were straight from my grandfather's mouth.

On Succot, my grandfather never slept in the *succa*. Everyone in the family, male and female, had to make the blessing on the four species. We ate in the succa on Shmini Atzeret. During Hallel, verses were repeated without the *"hodu la-ha-Shem."* As for the waving of the four species during the *na'anuim*, he stood in one place without turning his body—only the lulav, etc., were waved in the many directions.

On Passover, my grandfather drank four cups of wine despite the fact that he could not tolerate alcohol. It is one of the examples of being strict with himself while always finding an easier way for everyone else. He also took a long time to say the *Shmone Esrei*, constantly telling the congregation not to wait for him, for he did not want to be a burden on the community. But they always waited out of respect nonetheless.

My grandfather ate the largest *ke-zayit* possible of shmura matza on Passover. Considering that the matza in Brisk was really thick, this was no easy task. Maror was not sliced, but grated, and *maror* was always horseradish. No *matza ashira* was eaten.

We always said, in addition to the usual four questions, a fifth question in addition to the question on dipping the food: The question comes from the time of the Temple: on all other nights we eat roasted, preserved, and boiled meat; why on this night do we only eat roasted meat?

With encouragement from his mentor, Dr. Pinchas Churgin of Yeshiva University, and his wife, my father completed his B.A. at Yeshiva University in 1942. He had only needed a couple of semesters to add to his three years' work at Hebrew University to complete the degree, but until then had not had the patience to take care of them. The arguments in favor of his finishing were that he would be able to advance in his career and earn more money. He was the only one in his class to not only be married, but to also be a father. He earned his B.A. while working on his doctoral dissertation. His topic was "A Critical Edition of *Ma'alot ha-Midot*." Written in Italy by Rabbi Yechiel ben Yekutiel Anav, it was a book on ethics, and therefore, according to Dr. Churgin, a relatively easy topic for my father, who had been so immersed in the *musar* movement of Slobodka Yeshiva. He earned his doctorate in 1946. By this time he had three children.

Until that time, my father had been teaching, first in the Teachers' Institute for Women of Yeshiva University (1935-38) and the Teachers' Institute for Men of Yeshiva University (1938-46). Earlier he had taught at Etz Hayim and Shulamith High School, both in Brooklyn. Once he obtained his teaching diploma in 1935, he began to move up the ladder to these teachers' institutes. With the title "Doctor," he was appointed director of the Hebrew Teachers' Institute of Canada, located in Montreal, where he served from 1946 to 1951.

For both personal and professional reasons, my father then returned to New York and was given the position of instructor of Hebrew literature at the Teachers' Institute of Yeshiva University. In 1956, he was offered the more prestigious position of Instructor of Bible at Yeshiva College. He was promoted to assistant professor of Bible in 1963, and to associate professor in 1968. His promotions were based only on his outstanding teaching, as he published nothing in all of these years. He remained an associate professor until he was forced to retire in 1974 because of Yeshiva University's mandatory age retirement policy. He fought to keep his position, but lost.

In his forty years at Yeshiva University, my father taught thousands of students. They all remember his passion for the Prophets, his stress on the Hebrew language, and his personality.

The last decade of his life was spent in Jerusalem, where he moved with my mother in 1975. Periodically he would meet old classmates, colleagues, and students. If the latter, they would start declaiming verses from Isaiah or Amos that they had memorized in his classes. I have the same experience even now when I meet his previous students. On his tombstone there is a Hebrew inscription: "R. Moshe Aron ben Rav Simcha Zelig and Sara—"Moreh le-mofet; 'arba'im shana sheret" (An exemplar of an educator—he served for forty years).

Simcha Zelig Reguer (variations on the last name: Ryjer, Riger, Rieger, Rijer) was born in Navorodok in 1863. His father, Rav Dov, was part of Volozhin Yeshiva. His brilliance was evident at a very young age. When he entered Volozhin Yeshiva, he was befriended by Rav Haim Soloveitchik, who, when offered the rabbinate in Brest-Litovsk, agreed to serve only if Rav Simcha Zelig became the *dayyan* of the city. The two families lived in the same two-family house until World War I, when the men separated. After the war, Rav Simcha Zelig returned to Brest-Litovsk, but now Rav Velvel Soloveitchik was rabbi.

He married Sara (Sorke) Rudensky at the age of twenty-one. They had seven children who lived to adulthood: three sons and four daughters. The two older sons became socialists, as did the youngest daughter. Two daughters married and stayed in Brest-Litovsk. The third son, Moshe Aron, is the author of this memoir.

Rav Simcha Zelig was the Rosh Av Bet Din of Brest Litovsk and a main legal decisor for decades. He was known for being a *maikil*, working in the so-called "gray area" of Jewish law. Very few of his legal decisions were published. The most famous one had to do with the use of a refrigerator on Shabbat. He gave *smicha* to many rabbis, including Rav Isser Yehuda Unterman and Rav Joseph DovBer Soloveitchik.

Despite obtaining a visa for the United States, Rav Simcha Zelig decided to remain in Brest-Litovsk when World War II began. He was executed by the Nazis in October 1942, the third of MarCheshvan, along with the rest of the Jewish men of the city.

My father found eighteen references to my grandfather in a variety of publications and reprinted them in Moshe Avraham Landy, ed., *Giyon Maharsha: Bava Metzia* by Shlomo Eiger (Jerusalem: Zohar, 1983), 201-208.

Biography of Moshe Aron Reguer

Moshe Aron Reguer was born in Brest-Litovsk in November 1903, the youngest son of Rav Simcha Zelig and Sara Reguer. He was educated in a variety of *cheders* and by private tutors until World War I, when he studied in Volozhin, then Bobruisk, and then Rav Meltzer's yeshiva in Slutzk. In 1917, he traveled to Kremenchug in Ukaraine to join the Slobodka Yeshiva headed by "Der Alter," Rabbi Finkel. He remained there and in its satellite yeshiva in Karilov until 1920, when the yeshiva left Ukraine, heading north to return to Slobodka, a suburb of Kovna. In 1921/2 he studied in Takhkemoni Yeshiva in Bialistok, but when R. Polachek left for America, he transferred to the Warsaw branch, where he remained for a number of years. In 1925 he joined the Zionist movement, trained on an agricultural farm, and left for British Mandatory Palestine in 1926 to study in Hebrew University. In 1929 he obtained his British-Palestinian citizenship, and left for America on a student visa, endorsed by Yeshiva University. There he earned his BA, and in 1946 his Doctorate of Hebrew Letters.

Dr. Reguer married Anne Shabasson in 1936, and they had three children—Gabriel, Sara, and Simcha Zelig. He taught at Yeshiva University until 1974, when he retired and moved to Israel. He died in 1985.

Rabbinic Figures

Balaban, Dr. Meir (1977-1942). Historian, educator, writer. Founder of Takhkemoni Yeshiva centered in Warsaw, with a branch in Bialystok. Professor of Jewish history at the University of Warsaw.

Berlin, Rabbi Naftali Tzvi Yehuda (Netziv, 1816-1893). Head of Volozhin Yeshiva from 1853 until its closure by the Russian government in 1892. Brilliant scholar and legal decision maker.

Finkel, Rabbi Natan Tzvi (Der Alter, 1849-1927). Founder of Slobodka Yeshiva. An adherent of the *musar* movement, he was also known for upgrading the post of *mashgiach*. His branch of the Slobodka Yeshiva, Knesset Yisrael, survived World War I by moving to Kremenchug, Ukraine, and returned to Slobodka after the war.

Heiman, Rabbi Shlomo (the Pritzi, 1892-1947). Rabbi, talmudist, rosh yeshiva. Taught in Kaminetz Yeshiva Beis Yitzchok in exile in Kremenchug during World War I. After the war, he became rosh yeshiva of Ramailles until 1935, when he moved to New York to head Mesivta Torah Vadaath. Married Feigl Rudensky, niece of Rav Simcha Zelig Reguer.

Horwitz, Rabbi Yosef Yozl (1847-1919). Student of Rav Yisrael Salanter, as well as other rabbis. Established the Navorodok yeshiva, which taught an extremist form of *musar*. Known for living alone in a forest retreat for twelve years, practicing what he preached.

Meltzer, Rabbi Isser Zalman (1870-1953). Rabbi of Slutzk, Rosh Yeshiva of Etz Haim Yeshiva.

Polachek, Rabbi Shlomo (Meitscheter Illui, 1877-1928). Educated in Volozhin Yeshiva until it closed in 1892, then went with his mentor, Rav Chaim Soloveitchik, to Brisk. Transferred to Slobodka, then appointed rosh yeshiva, first in Lida, then in Takhkemoni in Bialysotk, and finally in Rabbi Itzhak Elchanan Seminary in New York City.

Schatz, Boris (1867-1932). Lithuanian Jewish artist. Ardent Zionist who founded the art center in Jerusalem known as Bezalel in 1906.

Shach, Rabbi Elazar (the Vaboilnik, 1899-2001). In 1909 went to study in Ponevezh Yeshiva, and then in Slobodka's Knesset Israel until World War I. For a while was in Slutzk where he was influenced by Rabbi Meltzer. Worked in many different yeshivot until the outbreak of World War II, when he escaped to Palestine. Eventually he became the head of Ponevezh yeshiva in Bnai Brak, Israel.

Shapira, Rabbi Refael (1837-1921). Rosh yeshiva of Volozhin until it closed in 1892. Son-in-law of the Netziv. Father of Livsha (wife of Rav Haim Soloveitchik).

Soloveitchik, Rabbi Haim (1853-1918). Rosh yeshiva of Volozhin from 1880 until it closed in 1892, when he became rabbi of Brest-Litovsk. Outstanding talmudist of his age.

Soloveitchik, Rabbi Moshe (1876-1941). Son of Rav Chaim, served in a number of rabbinic positions including in the Warsaw Takhkemoni Yeshiva before moving to New York to Rabbi Itzhak Elchanan Seminary. Father of Rabbi Joseph Dov Ber Soloveitchik.

Soloveitchik, Rabbi Velvel (Yitzhak Ze'ev, 1886-1960). Son of Rav Chaim, inherited his father's position in Brest-Litovsk. Escaped the Nazis in 1941, settled in Jerusalem.

Spektor, Rabbi Yitzhak Elhanan (1817-1896). Served as rabbi in many communities in the Russian Empire, most importantly Kovno. Was known also for his diplomacy and for trying to get all Jews to work together, including early Zionists.

Unterman, Rabbi Isser Yehuda (1886-1976). Educated in Etz Chaim Yeshiva, pupil of Rav Shimo Shkop. Ordained by Rav Simchah Zelig Reguer and by Rav Raphael Shapiro. In 1924 he moved to Liverpool, and was an active Zionist. In 1946 he became chief rabbi of Tel Aviv, and then chief Ashkenazi rabbi of Israel in 1966. His second wife was Feigl Rudensky Heiman.

Family Members

Chaim Reguer (1889-1977). Oldest surviving son of Rav Simcha Zelig and Sorke. Emigrated to New York before World War I and joined US armed forces. Lived the rest of his life in New York City.

Esther Reguer (1900-1942). Third daughter of Rav Simcha Zelig and Sorke. Married Zalman Chary, a wealthy businessman, had 3 daughters, and died with all of them in October 1942 in Brest-Litovsk.

Feigl Reguer (1896-1942). Oldest daughter of Rav Simcha Zelig and Sorke. Married Rabbi Moshe Reuven Gulewski during World War I. Had one daughter and one son. Died with the other women of Brest-Litovsk in October 1942.

Golde Reguer (1898-1959). Second daughter of Rav Simcha Zelig and Sorke. Moved to New York and married Moshe Ginsberg. Had one daughter.

Peshke Reguer (1908-1942). Youngest child of Rav Simcha Zelig and Sorke. Moved to Warsaw and married Aron Yeshonovitz. Had one son. Killed with her family in Brest-Litovsk in October 1942.

Shimon Reguer (1891-1976). Second surviving son of Rav Simcha Zelig and Sorke. Moved to the United States. Married and had two children.

Sara [Sorke] Rudensky Reguer (1861-1938). Daughter of Rabbi Abraham and Rotke Rudensky. Married Rav Simcha Zelig in 1884. Had seven children who reached adulthood. Spent most of her life in Brest-Litovsk.

Feigl Rudensky. Niece of Sorke. Married Rav Shlomo Heiman, and then Rav Isser Yehuda Unterman.

Moshe Reuven Gulewski (d.1942). Married Feigl Reguer, lived with Rav Simcha Zelig and Sorke until killed in October 1942.

Chaim Ber Gulewski (b. 1923). Son of Rav Moshe Reuven Gulewski and Feigl Reguer. Escaped the Nazis by travelling with the Mir Yeshiva to Japan and then to Shanghai. Travelled to the US after the war, married Yemima Chovav, had four children. Taught in Yeshiva University until he retired.

Anne [Chantche] Shabasson Reguer (1911-1979). Born in Poland, emigrated to Montreal after World War I, married Moshe Aron Reguer in 1936. Had three children. Lived most of her adult life in New York City.

www.ingramcontent.com/pod-product-compliance
Lightning Source LLC
Chambersburg PA
CBHW070410100426
42812CB00005B/1700